AF604874

# When Books Go Bad

# When Books Go Bad

## Tales of Literary Feuds, Publishing Errors and Withering Reviews

**Alex Johnson**

**Illustrations by Bill Bragg**

BRITISH LIBRARY

*To Phyllis and Philip,*
*Wilma,*
*Robert, Edward, and Thomas*

First published in 2025 by
The British Library
96 Euston Road
London NW1 2DB
bl.uk



Cataloguing in Publication Data
A catalogue record for this book is available from The British Library

ISBN 0 978 7123 5583 4

2 4 6 8 10 9 7 5 3 1

Represented in the EU by
Authorised Rep Compliance Ltd.,
Ground Floor, 71 Lower Baggot Street, Dublin, D02 P593, Ireland
www.arccompliance.com

Design and typesetting by Karin Fremer
Printed and bound in the Czech Republic by PBtisk

## *Contents*

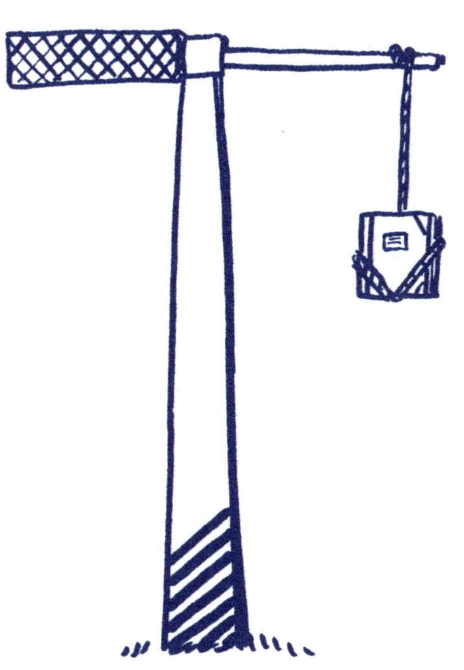

# INTRODUCTION

*Schlechte Bücher sind intellektuelles Gift;*
*sie verderben den Geist.*

'ÜBER LESEN UND BÜCHER', ARTHUR SCHOPENHAUER

*Bad books are intellectual poison;*
*they destroy the mind.*

'ON READING AND BOOKS', ARTHUR SCHOPENHAUER

**Books change lives**, writers confront us with sublime truths, literature makes life beautiful. Well, up to a point, Lord Copper. What happens when books go bad? Hardbacks poison us, authors murder us and libraries prevent us from wearing hats (see p. 148).

The truth is that the world of literature is a reflection of the wider world itself – yes, it has its finer moments and its distinguished practitioners, but it also has its crackpot critics and its book burners, its fakes and its feuds, its errors and its censors. And some of the fictional scoundrels in novels are only lightly disguised scoundrels found in real life.

The quality of writing itself is irrelevant in these cases. This book makes no evaluation of the literary worth of Edward 'It was a dark and stormy night' Bulwer-Lytton's prose, but does point out that he had his wife committed to a mental asylum because she heckled him a bit at one of his election hustings. *The Da Vinci Code* may or may not be your cup of tea, but what we're interested in here is Dan Brown's personal life.

Many areas of the literary world are covered in these pages. You'll find plenty of authors behaving badly, novelists lobbing insults and initiating feuds, and then taking the logical next step by physically grappling with each other using their fists, swords and pistols. There are romances that shocked society and books that have been lost to us through clumsiness, thievery or natural disaster (not to mention the ones you *really* shouldn't flick through). It's about publication errors and stinging book reviews, libraries warning against expectorating on the premises, and books you can use as weapons when your back's against the wall.

And if the mountain of things going wrong or the poor behaviour of Charles Dickens starts to get you down, remember Dr Johnson's comment on the proposition that once you've started a book you should read it through to the bitter end. 'This is surely a strange advice; you may as well resolve that whatever men you happen to get acquainted with, you are to keep them for life. A book may be good for nothing; or there may be only one thing in it worth knowing; are we to read it all through?'

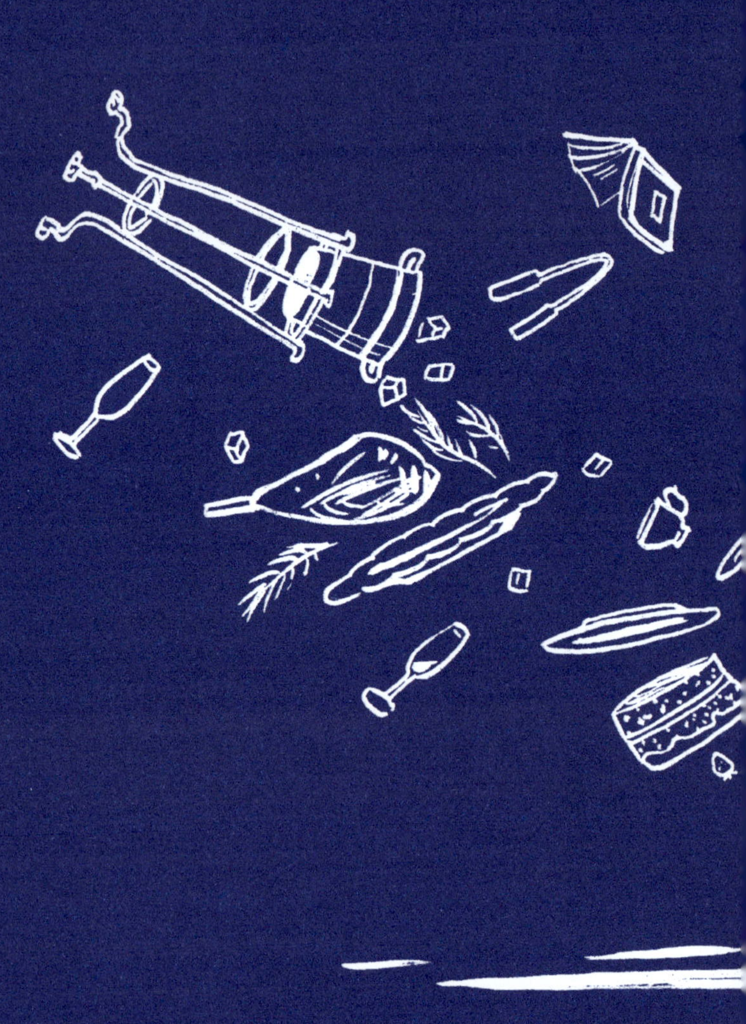

# Part I: PEOPLE

«1»

# AUTHORS

***All writers behave badly. All people behave badly.***

BIOGRAPHER CLAIRE TOMALIN,
INTERVIEWED IN THE *GUARDIAN*, 2011

**The second of** October 1944 was a big day for Gwen Davies. During her hush-hush war work at Bletchley Park she had met and fallen in love with the Welsh poet Vernon Watkins, and on this date they were to be marrried in London. Not only that, but the even more famous Welsh poet Dylan Thomas, one of Vernon's best friends and whom she had yet to meet, was to be the best man. Indeed, five years earlier, the self-styled 'Rimbaud of Cwmdonkin Drive' had borrowed one of Vernon's suits to be best man at the marriage of poets Lynette Roberts and Keidrych Rhys.

Gwen's big day was consequently rather spoiled when Thomas didn't turn up to either the pre-wedding lunch or the church ceremony itself, and only apologised a month later by letter, claiming he had caught a taxi in good time, but simply forgotten the venue (Gwen believed he was simply too shy and didn't want to hang out with strangers – a more unkind person might wonder if alcohol had played any part).

Many writers have added an impressive variety of bad behaviour to their CVs. You can blame drink, you can blame deadline pressure, you can blame the zeitgeist, but by any standards novelist

David Foster Wallace throwing a coffee table at the writer Mary Karr is not right. Sometimes, though, one person's poor conduct is another person's lot of fuss about nothing.

In 1949, a few months before his death, George Orwell put together a list for the Information Research Department, a covert section of the Foreign Office. It featured more than 130 prominent people (overwhelmingly male, mostly British) who would not be suitable for helping with anti-communist propaganda because of their political and social beliefs. Once it was made publicly known, the general feeling was summed up by writer Alexander Cockburn, who described it as a 'snitch list'. While much of the information about those with left-leaning sympathies – such as playwright and novelist J.B. Priestley and historian E.H. Carr – can hardly have been news to the IRD, Orwell's additional comments, such as 'tendency towards homosexuality' (poet Stephen Spender) and 'very anti-white' (singer Paul Robeson), do not do him credit.

But not everybody has seen it as such a terrible thing. The journalist Christopher Hitchens argued that commentators had gone overboard over an essentially 'trivial episode' which, rather than being a smear job, centred on recruiting appropriate campaign supporters rather than building dossiers for McCarthy-like investigation. Whatever your thoughts, though, the optics of handing over a list of names to a secret government department of people to keep an eye on are not great.

If the importance of Orwell's list is still up for debate, other authors' attitudes are more patently disagreeable. On the plus side, L. Frank Baum, best known for the *Wizard of Oz* series of books, was a supporter of the women's suffrage movement in the United States. On the down side, he also wrote a couple of newspaper articles in 1890 and 1891 calling for the genocidal extinction of Native Americans. While some have suggested that it was done sarcastically or that in fact he respected them so much that he felt it would be more noble to allow them a dignified death rather than eke out a miserable existence, it's hard to really get behind anybody who wrote this:

> *The proud spirit of the original owners of these vast prairies inherited through centuries of fierce and bloody wars for their possession, lingered last in the bosom of Sitting Bull. With his fall the nobility of the Redskin is extinguished, and what few are left are a pack of whining curs who lick the hand that smites them. The Whites, by law of conquest, by justice of civilization, are masters of the American continent, and the best safety of the frontier settlements will be secured by the total annihilation of the few remaining Indians. Why not annihilation? Their glory has fled, their spirit broken, their manhood effaced; better that they die than live the miserable wretches that they are.*

A century later, Roald Dahl's reputation as one of the leading children's writers of the late twentieth century took a substantial hit when it appeared he was happy to regard himself as an anti-Semite, unwisely going so far as to assert in an 1983 interview for the *New Statesman* that 'even a stinker like Hitler didn't just pick on them for no reason'. It's not hard to see why it became necessary for the Roald Dahl Story Company and Roald Dahl Museum to apologise for 'the lasting and understandable hurt caused' and his 'undeniable and indelible' racism.

Consequently, his books also came under fire, with the same accusations of misogyny and racism that were levelled at him personally examined in his texts– for example, critics argue that the Oompa-Loompas in *Charlie and the Chocolate Factory* are essentially African slaves. So fierce was the uproar that in 2023 his publishers Penguin made significant changes to many of Dahl's books, which were themselves then also hotly contested: novelist Salman Rushdie criticised them as 'absurd censorship' while acknowledging that Dahl was 'no angel'. Similar charges were made about Enid Blyton's work – variously that it was sexist, xenophobic and racist – and her publishers made equally drastic changes. Dr Seuss Enterprises went a step further. Following an examination of the *Cat in the Hat* author's oeuvre in 2021, it decided to withdraw six books from publication, saying: 'These books portray people in ways that are hurtful and wrong.' One result of which was that sales of *And to Think That I Saw It on Mulberry Street* went through the roof.

Authors are not universally recognised for being marvellous with money. Dr Samuel Johnson was arrested twice for debts (£5 in 1756, and a more substantial £40 two years later), briefly spending time in a debtors' prison. Naturally, he had some thoughts on the subject. 'Small debts are like small shot,' his biographer Boswell recorded him saying; 'they are rattling on every side, and can scarcely be escaped without a wound: great debts are like cannon; of loud noise, but of little danger.' He was also rather defensive about exactly whose fault debt was, adding: 'Those who made the laws have apparently supposed that every deficiency of payment is the crime of the debtor. But the truth is, that the creditor always shares the act, and often more than shares the guilt, of improper trust.'

The prolific pamphleteer and *Robinson Crusoe* creator Daniel Defoe was certainly not to be trusted with your life savings, even though he was also a ground-breaking business writer. Before he embarked on his chronicle of the famous shipwrecked slave trader (in hindsight, also a poor choice of profession for a hero), he dabbled in all sorts of entrepreneurial opportunities: marine insurance, wine imports, diving bells, farming civet cats (to make perfume) and brick-making. In 1692, he was committed to King's Bench Prison in London because he was indebted to around 140 creditors who were owed the then astronomical figure of £17,000, around the £3 million mark in today's money. It's perhaps pertinent that Crusoe himself laments that 'my head began to be full of projects and undertakings beyond my reach, such as are, indeed, often the ruin of the best heads in business'. Defoe was bankrupted twice and like Dr Johnson spent time in debtors' prisons, pursued by his creditors right up until his death.

Two hundred years later across the Atlantic, William Porter – the American short-story writer known as O. Henry who produced the classic Christmas tearjerker 'The Gift of the Magi' – was sent down for embezzlement while working at the First National Bank of Austin. Although he claimed he was innocent, he rather ruined that defence by also legging it to Honduras. Originally sentenced to five years in 1898, he got out two years early thanks to good behaviour.

Pinching other people's money is one thing. Killing them is quite another. The poets Paul Verlaine and Arthur Rimbaud had a particularly fiery romantic relationship which came to a definitive halt when Verlaine intended to prevent Rimbaud from dumping him by snatching a gun, shouting 'I'll teach you to leave,' and shooting. Fortunately for all involved, he only hit Rimbaud's wrist, but was still sentenced to two years in prison. Here are four writers who went a fatal step further:

## William Burroughs

One of the leaders of the Beat Generation and the author of *Naked Lunch* was convicted of the manslaughter of his partner, Joan Vollmer Adams, in Mexico. Both had an unfortunate relationship with drugs and alcohol and in 1951, after they had both had a few drinks, she unwisely took him up on his suggestion of playing a William Tell game with his gun. Placing a glass on her head, Burroughs took a shot and fired too low, killing her, though he later changed his story and claimed the gun had in fact fallen out of his hand and just gone off. He skipped the country and returned to his native US. In his absence, he was convicted of manslaughter. Norman Mailer came perilously close to doing something comparable when he drunkenly stabbed his wife Adele Morales, twice, with a pen knife after she shouted at him, 'Come on, you little faggot, where's your cojones?' Happily, she survived after two days in intensive care. Remarkably, she didn't press charges.

## Anne Perry

The multimillion-selling detective fiction writer Anne Perry (born Juliet Hulme), known for her popular Victorian husband-and-wife team Charlotte and Thomas Pitt as well as her William Monk series, was convicted in New Zealand in 1954 when she was fifteen of murdering her friend Pauline Parker's mother. The events were dramatised in Peter Jackson's film *Heavenly Creatures*. After five years in prison and a change of name, she moved to England and then settled in Scotland, publishing her first novel in 1979, *The Cater Street Hangman*. Perry died in 2023, aged eighty-four.

### Nancy Crampton-Brophy

Probably the least well known on this list, self-published romance novelist Crampton-Brophy made the schoolgirl error of writing a detailed blog post called 'How to Murder Your Husband' before proceeding to do just that seven years later in a bid to get a £1 million life insurance payout. Convicted of murder in 2022 and currently serving a life sentence, she was also the author of a novel called *The Wrong Husband*. Cybill Shepherd played her in the inevitable 'based on real events' film of the incident.

### François Villon

France's finest medieval poet is perhaps best known among English-speakers for his line '*Mais où sont les neiges d'antan?*', translated into English by Dante Gabriel Rossetti as 'Where are the snows of yesteryear?' (and quoted in the original French in an episode of *Downton Abbey* by Dame Maggie Smith's character, the Dowager Countess of Grantham). Villon was also no stranger to law-breaking. Born in 1431, he got caught up in various robberies and thefts until he disappeared from the historical record in 1463. He also stabbed and murdered a priest, arguably in self-defence, in 1455 in Paris. His death sentence was commuted to banishment from the city and eventually he received a royal pardon before a theft of gold coins from the university brought him a second banishment.

Even if you don't kill anybody, you can still go to prison. Nelson 'The Man With the Golden Arm' Algren got five months for pocketing a typewriter, Chester 'A Rage in Harlem' Himes spent eight years inside for armed robbery, and Beat poet Gregory Corso was incarcerated for the theft of a suit from a tailor's shop. Short-story writer and novelist Richard Brautigan even deliberately got himself arrested in 1955 by throwing a brick through the local police station's window in order to make sure he had somewhere to spend the night and something to eat.

But in some cases it's debatable if the accusation of being a rotter is simply a case of being on the 'wrong side'. Russian novelist Fyodor Dostoyevsky, for instance, was found guilty of reading/circulating prohibited political writings and being a member of an active revolutionary group in 1849 – his sentence of death by firing squad was only rescinded at the very last minute by Tsar Nicholas I, though he was sent to Siberia and spent a decade in shackles and military service. Irish playwright Brendan Behan was another whose political leanings got him into trouble. He joined the IRA as a teenager and was given three years in borstal for planning to blow up Liverpool Docks, and then sentenced to fourteen years for the attempted murder of a policeman in 1942.

Behan was also partial to a drop of whiskey, which did not always improve his behaviour. In June 1956 he took part in an infamous interview with Malcolm Muggeridge for the BBC's *Panorama* programme. He was drunk when he turned up, carried on drinking when he arrived, and kicked off his shoes during the interview, which opened with him saying he needed to go to the toilet and ended with him singing 'The Auld Triangle', a song about prison life featured in his recent celebrated play *The Quare Fellow*. Sadly, the BBC has 'lost' the tape recording of the eventful episode, but it did have a tangible effect – when the newspapers reported what had happened the following day, half a dozen theatres showed keen interest on putting on *The Quare Fellow* in the West End. 'One drunken, speechless television appearance brought more of the things he wanted, like money and notoriety and a neon glory about his head, than any number of hours with a pen in his hand,' commented Muggeridge when he wrote about it in the *Observer* in 1970.

A full account of authors behaving badly when drunk would make a hefty volume, but special mention should be made of F. Scott Fitzgerald. One of his peccadillos when he was in his cups was throwing things at people. In her memoir *Cast of Thousands*, Anita Loos recounts a dinner at his house with his wife, Zelda, when he announced that he was going to kill both women, throwing at them from close range two large lit candelabras, a water jug, a metal wine cooler and a silver platter with a leg of lamb on it. On other occasions he threw ashtrays, wineglasses and figs at fellow dinner-party guests.

However, many writers reserve their finest examples of misconduct for their peers, as we shall see in the next chapter …

«2»

# INSULTS

*To tea, Teddy Chanler and Scott Fitzgerald, the novelist (awful).*

EDITH WHARTON, DIARY ENTRY FOR 5 JULY 1925

**Insulting other writers** has a long and ignoble history. Although he was hugely popular, the fifth-century BC playwright Euripides was also the brunt of various insults, especially by his fellow writer Aristophanes, who derided his mother as a vegetable seller, the same kind of 'That's your mum, that is'-style insult used in Rob Newman and David Baddiel's 'History Today' sketches two millennia later.

Indeed, the bigger they are, the harder they fall. The first contemporary printed reference that we have about William Shakespeare comes in 1592 when his fellow playwright Robert Greene published a pamphlet called *Greenes Groats-Worth of Witte bought with a Million of Repentance*. Within a morality story about the life of two brothers, Greene weaved gossipy and disparaging references to other writers of his day. It's not entirely clear who he was taking aim at, but probably Christopher Marlowe and even more likely a young Will Shakespeare, writing: 'There is an upstart Crow, beautified with our feathers, that with his Tygers hart wrapt in a Players hyde supposes he is as well able to bombast out a blanke verse as the best of you: and beeing an absolute Johannes factotum is in his owne conceit the onely Shake-scene in a countrey.'

Here are some examples of more modern, but still satisfyingly straightforward, verbal abuse:

'Gertrude Stein's prose-song is a cold black suet-pudding. We can represent it as a cold suet-roll of fabulously reptilian length. Cut it at any point, it is the same thing: the same heavy, sticky, opaque mass all through and all along.'

*British writer, critic and Vorticist Wyndham Lewis on American author Gertrude Stein*

'A village explainer. Excellent if you were a village, but if you were not, not.'

*Stein herself on Ezra Pound*

'A poor dotty Irishman ... he wrote absolute rot, you know. He began writing quite well and ... you could watch him going mad sentence by sentence. If you read *Ulysses*, it's perfectly sane for a little bit, and then it goes madder and madder.'

*Evelyn Waugh on James Joyce in a BBC television interview for Monitor, which can be found online*

'Very poor stuff. I think he was mentally defective.'

*Waugh again, this time on Marcel Proust*

'Wordsworth was a tea-time bore, the great Frost of literature, the verbose, the humourless, the platitudinary reporter of Nature in her dullest moods.'

*Dylan Thomas on William Wordsworth*

'An idiot child screaming in a hospital.'
*H.G. Wells on George Bernard Shaw*

'An enthusiasm for Poe is the mark of a decidedly primitive stage of reflection.'
*Henry James on Edgar Allan Poe*

'like a large shaggy dog just unchained scouring the beaches of the world and baying at the moon.'
*Robert Louis Stevenson on Walt Whitman*

'All raw, uncooked, protesting.'
*Virginia Woolf in her diary on Aldous Huxley*

There's a line, not always an awfully fine one, between criticism and abuse. Raymond Chandler was open about his reservations when it came to British detective fiction, outlining them in a finely articulated 1944 article for *Atlantic Monthly*, 'The Simple Art of Murder'. Sherlock Holmes, he argued, 'is mostly an attitude and a few dozen lines of unforgettable dialogue'. The solution to Agatha Christie's *Murder on the Orient Express*, he added, was 'guaranteed to knock the keenest mind for a loop. Only a half-wit could guess it.' And in a private letter to mystery critic James Sandoe, Chandler even went a bit further, describing Dorothy L. Sayers' *Gaudy Night* as 'sycophantic drivel ... How silly can you get?'

Sometimes that line is decidedly crossed. In a piece for the *New Yorker* in 2012, novelist Jonathan Franzen did a full-on hatchet job on Edith Wharton. Although he admired her actual work, such as *The Age of Innocence*, he took aim at Wharton the person on the basis that she was very rich, enjoyed gardening and toured Europe in a yacht. He also commented that her 'one potentially redeeming disadvantage' was that 'she wasn't pretty', going on later to suggest that 'Edith Wharton might well be more congenial to us now, if alongside her other advantages, she'd looked like Grace Kelly or Jacqueline Kennedy'.

Also inexcusable was French poet Charles Baudelaire's potshot at George Sand. To say 'Elle est bête, elle est lourde, elle est bavarde' ('She is dumb, she is clumsy, she is a chatterbox') is a bit much, but to go on to add 'Que quelques hommes aient pu s'amouracher de cette latrine, c'est bien la preuve de l'abaissement des hommes de ce siècle' ('That some men could fall in love with this latrine is proof of the decline of manhood in this century') is unpleasantly over the top. So was Friedrich Nietzsche's ungentlemanly description of her as 'diese fruchtbare Schreibe-Kuh' or 'this fertile writing cow'. And while we're on the subject of over-the-top insults, here's Lord Byron on John Keats: 'Here are Johnny Keats' piss-a-bed poetry … No more Keats, I entreat: flay him alive; if some of you don't I must skin him myself: there is no bearing the drivelling idiotism of the Mankin.' In an 1820 letter Byron also compared Keats unflatteringly to William Wordsworth and Samuel Taylor Coleridge, calling him 'a tadpole of the Lakes', but seems to have mellowed when Keats died young, describing him as 'a loss to our literature'.

Not a writer on everybody's lips today, Hannah More (1745–1833) was nonetheless an important literary figure of the day. A Bluestocking who used to hang out with Dr Johnson, she wrote plays and novels, opposed slavery, and was a philanthropist who helped to fund schooling for poor young girls. She was not universally popular, however. Among those who had their reservations was Liberal MP and Chief Secretary for Ireland Augustine Birrell. In his *Essays about Men, Women and Books* (1895), he wrote: 'You may search her nineteen volumes through without lighting upon one original thought, one happy phrase ... not a single expression of genuine piety, of heartfelt emotion, ever escapes her lips.' Even harsher, he added that she was 'one of the most detestable writers that ever held a pen' and 'flounders like a huge conger-eel in an ocean of dingy morality'. So strongly did Birrell feel about her work that he dug a large hole in his garden and buried all those nineteen volumes in it.

Not all insults are directed at individual writers. Martin Amis, in no mood to make new friends, said on the BBC's *Faulks on Fiction* television book programme that he would only ever write books for children if a brain injury compelled him to do so, going on to add that he 'would never write about someone that forced me to write at a lower register than what I can write'.

For whatever reason, some writers seem to bring out the worst in people. Two and a half centuries after her birth, Jane Austen's work is still hugely popular around the world. The rather less well-known today American man of letters Ralph Waldo Emerson was not a fan, though, commenting in the summer of 1861 (to be fair, only in his private notebooks rather than out loud) that her novels 'seem to me vulgar in tone, sterile in artistic invention, imprisoned in the wretched conventions of English society, without genius, wit, or knowledge of the world'. Nor was Charlotte Brontë keen on Austen, pronouncing herself simply 'puzzled' when a friend said they enjoyed *Pride and Prejudice* ('I should hardly like to live with her ladies and gentlemen, in their elegant but confined houses').

Mark Twain was rather more savage. 'Any library is a good library that does not contain a volume by Jane Austen. Even if it contains no other book.' Harsh, but quite witty. 'Everytime I read "Pride and Prejudice",' he wrote in an 1898 letter to Joseph Twichell, 'I want to dig her up and beat her over the skull with her own shin-bone.' Harsh, and needlessly violent.

Twain didn't just pick on Austen. Among his other putdowns was his reported comment on a novel by Henry James ('Once you put it down, you simply can't pick it up') and also the entire German language ('A verb has a hard time enough of it in this world when it's all together. It's downright inhuman to split it up. But that's just what those Germans do.'). And on fellow Austenophobe Emerson, he wrote to a friend in 1886 that the Transcendental essayist whom the mighty Walt Whitman referred to as his 'master' was not that hot on grammar, since 'it all at once arrests the flow of your serenity for a moment, like gravel in the bread'.

Of course Twain himself was not everybody's cup of tea. 'A hack writer who would not have been considered fourth rate in Europe, who tricked out a few of the old proven "sure fire" literary skeletons with sufficient local color to intrigue the superficial and the lazy,' was novelist William Faulkner's caustic verdict. Certainly, writers don't have to be contemporaries for one to dislike another. In 1947, 244 years after Samuel Pepys died, writer Harold Nicolson – the husband of novelist Vita Sackville-West – put down his thoughts about Pepys in his own diary. He described him as a 'mean little man' who was 'salacious in a grubby way' and like all good diarists had a 'little snouty, sneaky mind'.

Poet William Cowper put his criticism of fellow versifiers Alexander Pope and John Dryden rather more elegantly in a 1782 letter to his friend William Unwin. 'I admire Dryden most,' he starts off positively, before going on to add, 'who has succeeded by mere dint of genius, and in spite of a laziness and carelessness almost peculiar to himself.' Pope gets a similarly mixed comment: 'With the unwearied application of a plodding Flemish painter, who draws a shrimp with the most minute exactness, he had all the genius of one of the first masters. Never, I believe, were such talents and such drudgery united.'

Two and a half centuries later, when *The End of the Tour*, a biopic about David Foster Wallace, came out in 2015, Bret Easton Ellis gave it a balanced review on Medium, calling it a 'classy indie' but also noting it was overly reverential. In the same piece, he gave a similarly 'good news, bad news' verdict on the author generally, writing: 'I like David Foster Wallace even though I think for the most part he was a fake-out artist with a disingenuous persona ... Do I think he is the most overrated writer of my generation as well as the most pretentious and tortured? Yeah, I do ... Do I also think he was a genius? Yeah, I do.'

There are insults and then there are insults. When the first edition of the *Oxford English Dictionary* was finally completed after decades of work in 1928, a nine-course banquet was held at the Worshipful Company of Goldsmiths in London. Among the guests of honour was Prime Minister Stanley Baldwin, who gave a congratulatory speech to the 100 diners, all of whom were men. No women were invited, including Rosfrith Murray and Eleanor

Bradley, who had worked on the dictionary for more than twenty years. They were only invited to hang around in the minstrels gallery above. Lexicographer Agnes Carwell Fries said: 'It was explained to me that being "skied" meant that women could sit in the balcony above the hall and watch the men eat. I felt insulted and refused to go under those circumstances.'

Not all insults are intended, but that doesn't necessarily make them less insulting. On 19 October 1878, London socialite Mrs Richard Greville paid a call on George Eliot and her husband George Lewes during which she gave them a copy of Henry James's two-volume novel *The Europeans*. She visited them again two weeks later with James himself as her companion. As they left, Lewes regifted it to James, entirely unaware that he was the author of the novel, saying as he thrust the volumes at him: 'Take them away, please, away.'

'Our hosts hadn't so much as connected book with author, or author with visitor, or visitor with anything but the convenience of his ridding them of an unconsidered trifle; grudging as they so justifiedly did the impingement of such matters on their consciousness,' James later wrote in his 1917 book *The Middle Years*. 'The vivid demonstration of one's failure to penetrate there had been in the sweep of Lewes's gesture, which could scarcely have been bettered by his actually wielding a broom.'

It's not all one-way traffic. Sometimes the insultee hits back. The next chapter focuses on feuds but as a taster of what's to come, here's how Ernest Hemingway ('bells, balls and bulls,' said Vladimir Nabokov. 'Loathed it') and William Faulkner squared off.

In 1947 William Faulkner was asked during a visit to a creative writing class at the University of Mississippi to offer his top five living writers. He modestly put himself at number two, just behind Thomas Wolfe, but well above Ernest Hemingway at four, adding that the winner of the Nobel Prize in Literature 'has no courage, has never crawled out on a limb. He has never been known to use a word that might cause the reader to check with a dictionary to see if it is properly used.' Even John Steinbeck at five got less grief from him.

Faulkner didn't repeat this opinion in public, but four years later his comment did find its way into print in the summer 1951 issue of the *Western Review* published at the State University of Iowa. When Hemingway was made aware of it, he observed: 'Does he really think big emotions come from big words? He thinks I don't know the ten-dollar words. I know them all right. But there are older and simpler and better words, and those are the ones I use. Did you read his last book? It's all sauce-writing now, but he was good once. Before the sauce, or when he knew how to handle it.'

A little bit of tit-for-tat, but not arguably really a feud, as none of it happened face to face and it was more about the mechanics of writing than personal invective.

For a subtle yet still substantial attack, you can always turn to the index. In his excellent survey *Index, A History of the*, Dennis Duncan has various examples including J. Horace Round's index in his nineteenth-century tome *Feudal England*. He used it to excoriate his fellow historian and Professor of Modern History at Oxford Edward Freeman's work on the same issue with mentions of his peer at the back of the book such as 'when himself in error, 151', 'confuses individuals, 323–4, 386, 473', 'his pedantry, 334–9', 'misconstrues his Latin, 343, 436', and 'his special weakness, 388, 391'.

«3»

# FEUDS

*People can be friends. Writers, no.*
*Writers are condemned to hate one another.*

ISAIAH 'IZZY' THORNBUSH, IN *BECH AT BAY* BY JOHN UPDIKE

**It's not just** pop stars who have beef with each other: writers who are rivals have been at it hammer and quill for centuries. Dorothy Parker was certainly not averse to some feuding. Her memorable putdown of playwright and fellow feudee Clare Boothe Luce, who was holding the door of a hotel open for her, is one of the best-known one-liners on the planet: 'Age before beauty,' said Luce, indicating Parker should enter first. 'And pearls before swine,' said Parker, entering.

Even after her death she managed to get under the skin of her friend Lillian Hellman. Parker was a major supporter of civil rights in America and in her will, which also stipulated that she should be quietly cremated, left everything she owned to Martin Luther King Jr. Hellman, the executor of Parker's estate and hopeful of inheriting it too, was particularly incensed at being left out, as were all of Parker's relations. In retaliation for the perceived slight, she contested the will (unsuccessfully), chucked out most of Parker's books, papers and belongings, and sorted out a very public funeral service on the swanky Upper East Side. Hellman refused to claim her ashes.

Like many literary feuders, writer-philosophers Albert Camus and Jean-Paul Sartre were, a few not entirely congratulatory book reviews of each other's works aside, initially reasonably chummy, and Sartre's lover Simone de Beauvoir was quite jealous of the relationship. What tipped them over the edge was a gulf in their attitude to political morality. The pro-Stalin Sartre defended the Soviet leader's violent reign as justifiable means to a communist end. Camus, an advocate for peaceful socialism, felt exactly the reverse. In his 1951 non-fiction book *The Rebel*, about the history of revolution and rebellion in Europe, he argued that the revolution always ends in a repressively powerful and violent state, as it had done in the USSR. Sartre wrote a damning criticism in the French literary magazine *Les Temps modernes*. The issue sold tremendously well, the French media latched on to the pair's growing public row via an exchange of letters in which Sartre accused Camus of being naively unrealistic, and their friendship came to a decisively frosty end. It came to an even more decisive end when Camus died in a car crash in 1960 and Sartre continued the argument in a eulogy for him that again accused him of being stubbornly pure. In a private letter to a friend about the obituary, he called Camus 'a little crook from Algiers'.

A popular way of needling a nemesis is by throwing shade within actual works of literature. Alexander Pope managed to juggle numerous grudges, but worked especially hard on one with Colley Cibber, playwright, actor and poet laureate, a title celebrated by Pope with an epigram in his masterwork *The Dunciad*:

*In merry Old England, it once was the Rule,*
*The King had his Poet, and also his Fool.*

*But now we're so frugal, I'd have you to know it,*
*That Cibber can serve both for Fool and for Poet.*

In fact *The Dunciad* is full of anti-Cibber bile, such as Pope's takedown of his work as showing 'less human genius than God gives an ape'. The root of this hatred was a performance given by Cibber in a revival of the play *The Rehearsal* some years earlier in which he mocked onstage one of Pope's less successful plays, *Three Hours after Marriage*.

Cibber could give as good as he got, though. After holding his peace for many years, he ran out of patience in 1742 and wrote a short pamphlet, 'A Letter from Mr Cibber, to Mr Pope', in which he included a story about Pope visiting the largest prostitute available in a brothel in London, mocking his height (Pope stood 4 ft 6 ins tall), and recounting how 'I found this little hasty Hero, like a terrible *Tom Tit*, pertly perching upon the Mount of Love! But such was my Surprize, that I fairly laid hold of his Heels, and actually drew him down safe and sound from his Danger.' Cibber also refers to Pope's 'little-tiny Manhood'.

It's hard not to take criticisms of one's work personally. Despite a healthy and financially successful relationship with the Abbey Theatre in Dublin, which was partly under the control of co-founder playwright W.B. Yeats, when in 1928 Sean O'Casey submitted his new politically charged play *The Silver Tassie*, a row ensued. Neither Yeats nor his co-founder Lady Gregory was convinced that it was right for the Abbey, and they declined to put it on.

However, rather than send O'Casey a considered response, Lady Gregory simply forwarded Yeats's pretty forthright views on its unsuitability for performance. An incensed O'Casey then forwarded them in turn to the media, and the *Irish Times* published both them and the heated quarrel by correspondence that followed between Yeats (who called the play 'so much dead wood' and told the play's author rather combatively that 'you have never stood on its battlefields or walked its hospital') and O'Casey. It took seven years for tempers to cool down – O'Casey left Dublin partly as a result, and settled in England – and a rapprochement led to the play receiving its Irish premiere at the Abbey in 1935.

In 1871 Mark Twain generously credited his slightly younger mentor, playwright and journalist Bret Harte, for his big break. 'He trimmed and schooled me patiently,' he wrote, 'until he changed me from an awkward utterer of coarse grotesquenesses to a writer of paragraphs and chapters that have found a certain favor in the eyes of even some of the very decentest people in the land.' Harte gave Twain a reporting job when he was out of work, plus advice on his writing.

Then it all went very sour indeed. The main cause was Harte's request for a loan to see him through a lean period of writing when he was also hitting the bottle. Twain offered $25. Harte felt that an insultingly paltry response, and told Twain so. In addition he said he was not going to pay back the $750 he already owed Twain because the author of *Adventures of Huckleberry Finn* had given him some bad business advice on a previous project.

You can tell how well Twain took this from what happened when Harte was up for the post of US consul to Germany. Twain wrote a letter of protest to a friend whose wife was a cousin of US

President Rutherford B. Hayes. He pulled no punches. 'Harte is a liar, a thief, a swindler, a snob, a sot, a sponge, a coward, a Jeremy Diddler,' he wrote. 'He is brim full of treachery.' Most people would probably have stopped there, but for good measure Twain added: 'To send this nasty creature to puke upon the American name in a foreign land is too much.' Harte appears to have resisted the urge to hit back, despite Twain's ongoing hate campaign against him. Even Harte's death in 1902 didn't stop Twain. 'He was bad, distinctly bad; he had no feeling, and he had no conscience,' he wrote in his autobiography. 'He was an incorrigible borrower of money; he borrowed from all his friends; if he ever repaid a loan the incident failed to pass into history.'

One of the choicest ways of getting one over on a rival is to make his work look a fool too. While he was researching a biography of the poet Sir John Betjeman, A.N. Wilson was delighted to receive an unpublished letter by the poet laureate that indicated an adulterous love affair in 1944 with writer Honor Tracy which had been entirely kept under wraps, but was now being forwarded by a relative of Tracy's. Naturally he included it in the finished volume, but it was only when the book was published that it was pointed out to him that the letter included an acrostic – reading the first letter of each sentence in order revealed that 'A.N. Wilson is a shit'. It was a hoax, and one that Wilson tried to laugh off through gritted teeth. A week after the prank had been made public, Betjeman's previous biographer Bevis Hillier owned up, admitting he had been peeved by the advance publicity given to Wilson's book, and perhaps was also a bit upset about a bad review Wilson had given his own effort.

It was not perhaps the kind of feud to make the front pages, but *Nineteen Eighty-Four* and *Brave New World* provided their respective authors George Orwell and Aldous Huxley with plenty to chew over. Huxley was the pre-Orwell Eric Blair's French teacher at Eton whose dystopian novel came out in 1932. Scroll forward to 1946 and an article Orwell wrote for *Tribune* about Yevgeny Zamyatin's fictional futuristic totalitarian vision published in 1924, *We*. He compared the two, commenting that 'Zamyatin's book is less well put together' but adding that 'the resemblance with *Brave New World* is striking'. Moreover, he said: 'The first thing anyone would notice about *We* is the fact – never pointed out, I believe – that Aldous Huxley's *Brave New World* must be partly derived from it.'

Huxley denied it, saying that he'd never even heard of the book before he penned his own futuristic totalitarian vision, much less read it (over the years other texts have been identified as inspirations for Huxley, including H.G. Wells's *The First Men in the Moon*, while Kurt Vonnegut said in an interview for *Playboy* that 'I cheerfully ripped off the plot of *Brave New World*, whose plot had been cheerfully ripped off from Yevgeny Zamyatin's *We*').

In 1949, Huxley wrote to Orwell on the publication of the younger man's novel. Although largely complimentary, Huxley suggested his own take on the subject was much more realistic since 'whether in actual fact the policy of the boot-on-the-face can go on indefinitely seems doubtful. My own belief is that the ruling oligarchy will find less arduous and wasteful ways of governing and of satisfying its lust for power, and these ways will resemble those which I described in *Brave New World*.'

Another once cheery friendship gone for a Burton was that between H.G. Wells and Henry James. It started well enough, with James calling him 'the most interesting "literary man" of your generation'. It then went downhill when they disagreed about why literature was important (James was more of an artist, Wells a propagandist) and James, in typical Jamesian fashion, said in the *TLS* that Wells's work was full of 'affluents turbid and unrestrained'. It fully exploded when in 1915 Wells published *Boon*, a satirical novel that took direct aim at James. This included the memorable putdown of the writing style of a character inspired by James as a 'magnificent but painful hippopotamus resolved at any cost, even at the cost of its dignity, upon picking up a pea that has got into the corner of its den ... His vast paragraphs sweat and struggle.' They wrote a few letters back and forth which continued to stoke the fires, and then James died before they could make up.

When a writer has multiple feuds, questions have to be asked. As with James, George Orwell had been very positive about H.G. Wells's output, but then took against Wells's fascination with science, and their first meeting in London in the 1940s only made matters worse. Wells describing Orwell as 'an English Trotskyist writer with enormous feet' probably didn't help things.

One of the strangest incidents in this love–hate relationship was over a flat Wells was renting to George and his wife Eileen. The author of *The War of the Worlds* was invited over for dinner in 1941 in a bid to heal the rift, and while they had a robust discussion about how much of a threat the Nazis posed, he was offered a plate of curry. Initially reluctant, he then wolfed down plenty, and finished up with an impressive slice of plum cake. When Wells left that evening, it appeared that all was sweetness and light again, although the story goes that he wrote to them complaining that he had been on a diet, that they had known that, and still deliberately given him lots to eat and drink.

The following year Orwell went on the attack again, this time in a BBC radio broadcast including Wells in a grouping of other well-known writers such as Arnold Bennett and A.E. Housman who he said had no understanding of anything outside England. Wells wrote Orwell a very much to-the-point note, saying Orwell had misrepresented his views on the effects of science – 'I don't say that at all. Read my early works, you shit' – and that he never wanted to see him again.

Orwell had the last word, writing Wells's obituary for the *Manchester Evening News* in August 1946, essentially saying that Wells's work had been going downhill since 1910 and that 'though he continued to write novels, the old magic was no longer in them'.

Perhaps saddest of all is when family members fall out. Sisters Antonia 'A.S.' Byatt and Margaret Drabble were apparently quite, well, 'spirited' towards each other as children, encouraged to be so in fact by their mother. Elements of autobiography in their novels – Drabble's mention of a family tea set seems to have upset Byatt – added to the not necessarily healthy competition between them. Byatt's 1967 novel *The Game* was a notable staging post, described by her sister as 'a mean-spirited book about sibling rivalry'. There was certainly a coldness between them, and in 2011 Drabble said the whole thing was 'irresoluble now. It's sad, but beyond repair.' However, media commentators on the relationship may have exaggerated the problems, which Drabble once dismissed as 'normal sibling rivalry'. Byatt argued on *Desert Island Discs* that the situation was 'terribly overstated by gossip columnists', and Drabble's husband Sir Michael Holroyd said: 'They ask when they will bury the hatchet, but the fact is they are both too busy to be wielding any hatchets.'

Truman Capote vs Gore Vidal is one of those feuds that feel a bit one-sided. Granted, Capote wasn't the entirely blameless party. 'I'm always sad about Gore, very sad that he has to breathe every day,' are not joyous words of love. However, on the other side of the quarrel there is a veritable flood of jealous acrimony occasioned by Capote's success, such as:

> 'I first met Truman at Anaïs Nin's apartment. My first impression – as I wasn't wearing my glasses – was that it was a colourful ottoman. When I sat down on it, it squealed. It was Truman.'
>
> [On Capote's death] 'A brilliant career move.'
>
> 'Capote I truly loathed. The way you might loathe an animal. A filthy animal that has found its way into the house.'

It was also bad blood that reached as far as the courtrooms. Capote suggested in an interview that Vidal had been booted out of the White House by Robert Kennedy for poor, drunken behaviour – which unfortunately for him was not true. In 1975, Vidal sued for the then astronomical amount of $1 million and only settled the case in 1983 when Capote apologised in writing.

Virginia Woolf and Arnold Bennett seem to have had an odd relationship, mixing professional and personal dislike with a grudging respect. In her diary in February 1924 Woolf writes about meeting Bennett, 'a lovable sea lion, with chocolate eyes, drooping lids, & a protruding tusk. He has an odd accent; a queer manner; is provincial; very much a character.' And herein lay part of the problem. Woolf regarded Bennett, by some distance the more commercially successful of the two at the time, as inferior because of their class differences. Meanwhile, he described her in a review of Woolf's *A Room of One's Own* as 'queen of the high-brows' while he was a self-confessed low-brow (though he did admit that 'it takes all sorts of brows to make a world').

Like the Drabble–Byatt relationship, it's interesting that Bennett wrote in his diary in 1929 that 'I have often been informed by the elect that a feud exists between Virginia Woolf and myself, and I dare say that she has received the same tidings. Possibly she and I are the only two lettered persons unaware of this feud ... One thing I have said of her: she can write.'

They disagreed over writing styles, Bennett championing realism, Woolf very much a modernist. Bennett also provocatively wrote a book of essays in 1920 about male and female writers, *Our Women*, in which he argued that women were simply not as clever or as creative as men. Unsurprisingly, Woolf took exception to this and rebutted it in her 1926 pamphlet 'Mr Bennett and Mrs Brown', in which she put the case for fiction's need to change with the times. She also has a proper go at Bennett's novel *Hilda Lessways*, in which character development is lost since 'we can only hear Mr Bennett's voice telling us facts about rents and freeholds and copyholds and fines'.

They met occasionally at dinner parties and get-togethers in London, including at H.G. Wells's home in November 1926. 'Both gloomy, these two,' Bennett wrote in his diary about Virginia and her publisher husband, Leonard. 'But I liked them both in spite of their naughty treatment of me in the press ... I really wanted to have a scrap with Virginia Woolf; but got no chance.' At another occasion Bennett wrote: 'Virginia is all right; other guests held their breath to listen to us ... She taunted me with believing her to be "refined". Well, if she isn't refined then I don't know who is.'

His review of Woolf's *Orlando* in the *Evening Standard* in November 1928 continued the disagreement. In the piece ('A Woman's High-Brow Lark'), he described the opening chapter as 'goodish' but said that 'the second chapter shows a startling decline and fall-off ... The succeeding chapters are still more tedious ... Her best novel, *To the Lighthouse*, raised my hopes of her. *Orlando* has dashed them and they lie in iridescent fragments at my feet.'

Once again, only death sundered the two. Woolf wrote in her diary the day after he died that his passing 'leaves me sadder than I should have supposed'. She went on to call him both 'a lovable genuine man ... glutted with success' and 'an old bore' with 'a shopkeeper's view of literature ... and the desire for hideous Empire furniture'. She ended the entry like this:

> *Queer how one regrets the dispersal of anybody who seemed – as I say – genuine: who had direct contact with life – for he abused me; and yet I rather wished him to go on abusing me;*

*and me abusing him. An element in life – even in mine that was so remote – taken away. This is what one minds.*

Comic writers A.A. Milne and P.G. Wodehouse, born within a couple of months of each other, were not only friends but also fellow cricketers playing for the amateur side Allahakbarries CC, which consisted of the finest literary talents of the day. Milne even invested in Wodehouse's stage production of his own novel, *A Damsel in Distress*. But the lighthearted broadcasts Wodehouse made in the early years of the Second World War while detained by the invading Nazis broke their relationship entirely.

Wodehouse's reputation took a major public hit, and even when he was exonerated it took decades to recover. Milne was one of his chief critics, attacking what he saw as Wodehouse's lack of responsibility (including a personal dig at his parenting abilities) in a letter to the *Daily Telegraph*, saying that he had 'encouraged in himself a natural lack of interest in "politics" – "politics" being all the things grown-ups talk about at dinner when one is hiding under the table. Things, for instance, like the last war, which found and kept him in America; and postwar taxes, which chased him back and forth across the Atlantic.'

In turn, Wodehouse commented: 'Nobody could be more anxious than myself … that Alan Alexander Milne should trip over a loose bootlace and break his bloody neck.' He also mocked the Christopher Robin figure and Winnie-the-Pooh in his novel *The Mating Sesason*, as well as a short story, 'Rodney has a Relapse' (which features a character called Timothy Bobbin and his father who uses him as source material …), and told the *Paris*

*Review* that 'I think he was a pretty jealous chap. I think he was probably jealous of all other writers'. The two never spoke to each other again.

What's nice to see is when writers kiss and make up. Literary rivals and the two stellar novelists of their time William Thackeray and Charles Dickens (one of the star recidivists of this book) showed a grudging admiration to each other, although their mutual friend Dr John Brown said that Dickens 'could not abide the brother so near the throne'. The difference in their class backgrounds – Thackeray much more middle-class than Dickens – was also a source of some antipathy. Things went downhill when Thackeray's *Vanity Fair* and Dickens's *Dombey and Son* came out at about the same time in 1848, both to considerable acclaim. '[Dickens] can't forgive me for my success,' wrote Thackeray, 'as if there were not room in the world for both of us.'

They properly fell out when Thackeray made a reference to Dickens's affair with the actress Ellen Ternan. At this point one of Dickens's disciples, the journalist Edmund Yates, wrote a series of newspaper and magazine articles attacking Thackeray, who in turn had Yates expelled from the Garrick Club in revenge. The novelists' froideur continued for years, until they bumped into each other at the Athenaeum Club in 1863 and made up. Thackeray died soon afterwards. Here is what Dickens wrote in the *Cornhill Magazine* as an obituary: 'We had our differences of opinion. I thought that he too much feigned a want of earnestness, and that he made a pretence of under-valuing his art, which was not good for the art that he held in trust. But, when we fell upon these topics, it was never very gravely, and I have a lively image of him in my mind, twisting both his hands in his hair, and stamping about, laughing, to make an end of the discussion.'

Here are three more feudships that had a happy ending:

### V.S. Naipaul vs Paul Theroux

1966: Novelists and travel writers Paul Theroux and V.S. Naipaul meet and a warm friendship develops.

1979: Theroux uses his deciding vote on the judging panel to prevent Naipaul's *A Bend in the River* from winning the Booker Prize, but does not initially make this public.

1997: Theroux notices in a catalogue of modern first editions that three of his books which he has inscribed personally to Naipaul 'with love' are for sale at $1,500 each. The friendship sours.

1998: Theroux publishes his memoir *Sir Vidia's Shadow: A Friendship across Five Continents* in which, among many brickbats, he suggests Naipaul is a coward and a skinflint.

2001: In a harsh review of Naipaul's new novel *Half a Life*, Theroux discusses the author's attacks on other writers as 'the sort of explosive abuse you get from someone whose Valium has worn off'.

2011: Novelist Ian McEwan brokers a peace deal in private in the green room at the Hay Festival. 'So that is the end to the literary feud,' said Lady Naipaul, his second wife.

## Julian Barnes vs Martin Amis

Novelists Martin Amis and Julian Barnes were good friends, working together on the books section of the *New Statesman* in the 1970s, and meeting up regularly to play each other at snooker. Both went on to write numerous successful books, but Amis believed the £300,000 advance negotiated for his 1995 novel *The Information* was too paltry so fired his agent Pat Kavanagh and hired a new one, Andrew 'The Jackal' Wylie, known for his uncompromising bargaining techniques. Unfortunately, Kavanagh was married to Barnes, who felt betrayed and wrote a letter to Amis detailing his displeasure, ending it resolutely 'Fuck off'. By the time of Amis's death in 2023 (fifteen years after Pat's) they had managed to resume civilities.

## Salman Rushdie vs John le Carré

It is 15 November 1997. The *Guardian* prints part of a speech by John le Carré complaining about accusations of anti-Semitism the previous autumn in the *New York Times Book Review*, where his latest book, *The Tailor of Panama*, has been reviewed. Things escalate quickly.

Three days later the newspaper prints a letter by Salman Rushdie in which he complains about Le Carré's failure to back him over *The Satanic Verses* incident, saying, 'It would be easier to sympathize with him had he not been so ready to join in an earlier campaign of vilification against a fellow writer.'

The next day, 19 November, the newspaper's letter page carries Le Carré's reply that 'Rushdie's way with the truth is as self-serving as ever'.

In 20 November's edition, Rushdie begins his response with 'I'm grateful to John le Carré for refreshing all our memories about exactly how pompous an ass he can be.'

The same day, essayist Christopher Hitchens's letter to the *Guardian* is also printed. 'John le Carré's conduct in your pages is like nothing so much as that of a man who, having relieved himself in his own hat, makes haste to clamp the brimming chapeau on his head,' he writes. If this sounds unlikely to end the confrontation, you'd be right, since this is exactly what Hitchens intended. Talking about it in 2011 to a *New York Times* reporter he said: 'This is the original confrontation over free speech, which goes back to the trial of Socrates. I therefore did my best to make sure that no compromise or kiss-and-make-up was thinkable. One's job on such occasions, when seeing the embers begin to cool, is to blow on them as hard as possible.'

It is now 21 November and it's Le Carré's turn again. 'Rushdie sneers at my language and trashes a thoughtful and well-received speech I made to the Anglo-Israel Association, and which the *Guardian* saw fit to reprint. Hitchens portrays me as a buffoon who pours his own urine on his head. Two rabid ayatollahs could not have done a better job.'

The next day, Rushdie rushes back into print. '"Ignorant" and "semi-literate" are dunces' caps he has skillfully fitted on his own head. I wouldn't dream of removing them.'

Then a period of calm until 2011, when Rushdie remarks that 'I wish we hadn't done it' and Le Carré writes in *The Times* that 'I too regret the dispute ... And if I met Salman tomorrow? I would warmly shake the hand of a brilliant fellow writer.'

«4»

# FISTICUFFS

*Rien ne nous plaît que le combat*
*mais non pas la victoire.*

*It is the fight alone that pleases us,*
*not the victory.*

BLAISE PASCAL, *PENSÉES*

**When insults are** not good enough and a full-on feud just doesn't cut the mustard, there's only one thing left to do. Fight.

'That's for what you said to Patricia,' shouted Mario Vargas Llosa (or something along those lines) as he punched Gabriel García Márquez in the face and knocked him down in February 1976 at a film premiere in Mexico City. Patricia was Llosa's wife, but despite numerous theories – mostly centring on Vargas Llosa's love life, perhaps including García Márquez's suggestion to Patricia to divorce Mario, maybe an argument between the two over Fidel Castro and Cuba – the reason for the punch-up has never been properly explained. It lasted until García Márquez's death in 2014.

However, when you think of macho brawling scribblers, the first person most people will come up with is Ernest. Two of Hemingway's finest punch-ups were with writer Max Eastman and poet Wallace Stevens. Eastman had the bad luck to meet Hemingway at their mutual editor Max Perkins's office in New York. Hemingway reminded Eastman of 'Bull in the Afternoon,' his recent review of *Death in the Afternoon* in which he said Hemingway 'too much protests his manhood' and called him out as an example of the 'literary style, you might say, of wearing false hair on the chest'. Hemingway complained, 'What do you mean accusing me of impotence?' then took off his shirt to display his chest hair. He then unbuttoned Eastman's shirt, underneath which was an entirely smooth chest. For good measure, Hemingway then picked up a book of Eastman's own essays, *Art and the Life of Action*, walloped its author on the nose, slapped him and wrestled him to the ground.

The *New York Times*'s account of the disturbance three days later reports that 'Max Eastman says he then threw Hemingway over a desk and stood him on his head in a corner', a claim vehemently denied by the bullfighting aficionado. 'He didn't throw anybody anywhere. He jumped at me like a woman – clawing, you know, with his open hands. I just held him off. I didn't want to hurt him. He's ten years older than I am.'

The copy of Eastman's essays in question was discovered in the Ransom Center's archives in 1988 with the inscription: 'This is the book I ruined on Max (the Prick) Eastman's nose, I sincerely hope he burns forever in some hell of his own digging. – Ernest Hemingway.'

Wallace Stevens also felt Papa Hemingway's forceful nature when he met Hemingway's sister Ursula at a party in Key West in 1936. He explained to her in no uncertain terms his low opinion of her brother. She returned home, and told Ernest. Ernie nipped straight out to the party and punched Stevens – fifteen years his senior – to the ground (more specifically, a puddle, according to some reports). Stevens got back to his feet and gave Hemingway a wallop to the jaw which apparently broke his hand in two places before Hemingway went to town on him ('gave him a good beating,' he wrote to his friend Sara Murphy), requiring medical attention and bed rest for the following five days. 'Anyway last night Mr Stevens comes over to make up and we are made up,' he continued in the same letter. 'But on mature reflection I don't know anybody needed to be hit worse than Mr S.'

Hemingway revelled in his reputation as a bit of a slugger. In 1954, he told *Time* magazine in an inteview that he and James '*Ulysses*' Joyce used to hang out together. 'We would go out to drink and Joyce would fall into a fight. He couldn't even see the man so he'd say, "Deal with him, Hemingway! Deal with him!"' It's a great story (it even made it into Hemingway's obituary in the *New York Times*), though the only mention of Joyce using Hemingway as a bodyguard is by Hemingway himself and by the time he told the world about it, Joyce had been dead for a decade – so the anecdote may be a little, shall we say, buffed up.

In 2002, Colson Whitehead reviewed Richard Ford's short-story collection *A Multitude of Sins* for the *New York Times Book Review*. He didn't like it, and he said so. 'Almost every story deals with adultery, invariably in one of two stages: in the final dog days of an affair, or in the aftermath of an affair. The characters are nearly indistinguishable.' Two years later, Ford spotted Colson at a party, walked up to him and said: 'I've waited two years for this. You spat on my book.' Then he spat on Whitehead, who creditably did not do likewise, but did remark, 'This wasn't the first time some old coot had drooled on me, and it probably won't be the last.' In 2017, Ford seemed unrepentant. 'I can tell you that, as of today,' he wrote in *Esquire* magazine, 'I don't feel any different about Mr Whitehead, or his review, or my response.'

Leading bookseller of the day Thomas Osborne certainly picked the wrong writer when he turned up at Dr Samuel Johnson's home in 1742, and asked where the heck was the manuscript he'd been promised, a catalogue of Robert Harley the Earl of Oxford's celebrated library, which Osborne had recently bought for the then vast sum of £13,000. Osborne, not known for his politesse, was greeted not with an apology but with Johnson going full Hemingway, taking up a large book which he used to whack Osborne to the floor.

Some tellers of the story suggested he used his own *Dictionary*, though that would have been tricky since Johnson didn't publish it until the following decade, and later accounts suggest it was actually a sixteenth-century Greek Bible. Indeed, it's hard to tell exactly what happened since it was a literary tale that seemed to grow in the telling.

John Hawkins in his *Life of Samuel Johnson* (1787) suggested that he 'felled his adversary to the ground, with some exclamation', which, he says, 'I will not venture to repeat.' Johnson's friend Thomas Tyers in the *Gentleman's Magazine* (1784) adds that having knocked him down, Johnson told him 'not to be in a hurry to rise, for when he did, he proposed kicking him down stairs'. In the same year, William Cooke's biography of Johnson had him 'aiming a blow at the Bookseller's head' which sent him sprawling on the floor. 'Mr Johnson, clapping his foot on his breast, would not let him stir, till he had exposed him in that situation; and then left him, with this triumphant expression: "Lie there, thou son of dullness, ignorance, and obscurity."'

The truth? Johnson's friend the diarist Hester Thrale recorded: 'I asked him the other day about his combat with that Osborne, how much of the story was true: "It was true," said he, "that I beat the fellow, and that was all; but the world so hated poor Osborne that they have never done multiplying the blows and increasing the weight of them for twenty years together."' And his most famous biographer James Boswell? 'The simple truth I had from Johnson himself. "Sir, he was impertinent to me, and I beat him. But it was not in his shop: it was in my own chamber."'

No priceless folio handy to weaponise? Then it must be a duel. Playwright Ben Jonson's case of going toe to toe is an early example of what could, unsurprisingly, happen during a bust-up. In 1598, Jonson was challenged to a duel by an actor, Gabriel Spenser (although we only have Jonson's word for this, and no clue as to the reason), who had already admitted a murder charge a couple of years earlier following a stabbing. Spenser took Jonson up on his request and they fought a duel in Hoxton, London. Spenser managed a palpable hit on Jonson's arm but Jonson managed more than that, fatally running him through on his right side. Jonson confessed to the crime at his Old Bailey trail, though pointed out that Spenser had fought with a longer sword, which feels like poor mitigation. He escaped the death penalty by pleading 'benefit of clergy', which meant he was allowed to go once he had:

1. recited the penitential Psalm 51, known as the *Miserere* ('Have mercy on me, O God')

2. forfeited some property

3. had the Tyburn 'T' branded on his left thumb

4. served a short sentence in Newgate Prison.

One of the finest feuds in Russia was nurtured between Leo Tolstoy and Ivan Turgenev, who were once perfectly amicable, despite Turgenev's delight in Western Europe and lack of religiosity, which put him at odds with Mr *War and Peace*. The main bone of contention arose in 1861, when Tolstoy referred to an illegitimate child Turgenev had fathered outside his marriage and her good deeds, which Tolstoy thought were just virtue signalling. Huffy letters were sent back and forth until Tolstoy challenged Turgenev to a duel (pistols). Here's how American diplomat and Russophile Eugene Schuyler, who knew both men, saw the incident in his posthumously published *Selected Essays* (1901):

> *On returning [home], Turguenief found two notes from Tolstoy; one an apology and sincere regret for what he had said; the other, that the insult given to him could only be wiped out in blood, and challenging him to come the next morning, between five and six o'clock, to a place mentioned, and kill each other without witnesses. Turguenief thereupon sent one of his friends to propose a regular duel according to code. But Tolstoy had already gone back to [his estate at] Yasnaya Polyana, and, when he was found, repeated his apologies and retracted his challenge.*

Schulyer then reports a letter Turgenev sent to a friend, Annenkof:

> *I have entirely and decisively quarrelled with Leo Tolstoy. The question of a duel hung on a hair, and at this moment the hair is not yet broken. The fault is mine: but it was all the result of an old hostility – an antipathy of our two natures. I have always felt sure that he hated me, and I can never understand why, nevertheless, he used to come back to me. I have been forced to keep my distance – then I have tried to approach him; and we were very near approaching each other with pistols in our hands. I have never liked him.*

Turgenev came over to Tolstoy's home for a birthday celebration in 1881. Tolstoy noted in his diary after Turgenev had performed a well-known dance for his children, 'August 22nd. Turgenev – Cancan. Sad.'

Another roughly contemporary physical confrontation that ended with a whimper rather than a bang followed critic Jean Lorrain's review of Marcel Proust's *Pleasures and Days*, in which he also implied that Proust was gay and was sleeping with novelist Lucien Daudet. Even though he was actually gay, Proust promptly demanded satisfaction in the form of a duel. In the three days running up to the big day, his friend Reynaldo Hahn noted in his diary that Proust showed considerable sangfroid.

So it was that on a rainy 5 February 1897, the pair met with their pistols and their seconds at a popular Parisian duelling spot, the forest of Meudon. Separated by twenty-five paces, Proust shot first and missed (probably deliberately), his bullet hitting the ground near Lorrain's foot. Lorrain then shot and missed (probably deliberately). They decided that everybody's honour had been satisfied and went home. Interested parties could read all about it in the newspapers the next day, including in *Le Figaro*. Proust himself wrote about the event seven years later in a letter to the critic and poet Robert de Montesquiou. A keen proponent of staying in bed all day to work, he told him, 'My only concern was that the duel wouldn't take place before noon. When I was told it would take place in the afternoon, I didn't care at all.'

Duels with less happy results for the writers involved were fought by Russian poets Mikhail Lermontov and Alexander Pushkin. Lermontov's duel, in July 1841, was a brief contest following a quarrel with his frenemy and fellow army officer Nikolai Martyov, who took advantage of Lermontov's refusal to fire his pistol by shooting him in the heart, killing him almost immediately. The site of the duel on the north-western slope of the Mashuk mountain in the North Caucasus is marked with a substantial monument to Lermontov.

Four years earlier, Lermontov had written a poem called 'Death of the Poet' after Pushkin, a serial duellist, was fatally injured in a duel. Pushkin's beef had been with the alleged (though never admitted or proven) lover of his wife Natalia, Georges-Charles de Heeckeren d'Anthès, a French officer serving in the Russian army. In the duel in deep snow in a small pine forest near St Petersburg, the two combatants were a mere ten steps from each other. D'Anthès shot first and hit Pushkin in the stomach. Pushkin's retaliation as he fell merely grazed his opponent's arm. He died two days later in bed at home.

Even winners of the highest literary awards get a whacking sometimes. Sinclair Lewis, who in 1930 became the first American novelist to win the Nobel Prize in Literature, was not universally loved. In his novel *Across the River and into the Trees* Ernest Hemingway mocked Lewis's severe childhood acne in a bar scene, describing an unnamed man who had 'a strange face like an over-enlarged, disappointed weasel or ferret. It looked as pock-marked and blemished as the mountains of the moon seen through a cheap telescope.' But Lewis was not a pushover.

In 1927, his wife Dorothy Thompson travelled through Russia to research her new book, *The New Russia*, which was published

the following year. Not long afterwards novelist and journalist Theodore Dreiser, who had been with her for part of the trip, published his own account, *Dreiser Looks at Russia*. Lewis and Thompson accused him of major plagiarism. Dreiser denied the charge, and indeed claimed Thompson must have pinched and used his own notes.

Things came to a head in 1931 when Lewis and Thompson bumped into Dreiser at a banquet held at New York's Metropolitan Club honouring the Russian writer Boris Pilnyak. Asked to make a speech of welcome, and perhaps slightly the worse for wear, Lewis declared: 'I feel disinclined to say anything in the presence of the son of a bitch who stole 3,000 words from my wife's book.' The banquet over, Dreiser approached him in the cloakroom and challenged him to repeat the allegation to his face. Lewis did so. Dreiser slapped him on the face and dared him to do it again. Lewis did so. Dreiser slapped him again. When he was restrained, Dreiser shouted: 'I'll meet you any time, anywhere. This thing isn't settled.' The media lapped it all up and referred to it as 'the slap heard round the world'.

Thanks to the white heat of technology, modern feuds are played out to a public audience like never before. Bellicose novelist Norman Mailer and intellectual man of letters Gore Vidal never saw eye to eye. 'My first reaction to *The Naked and the Dead* was: it's a fake,' Vidal said in a 1960 essay in the *Nation*, of Mailer's 1948 bestseller. 'A clever, talented, admirably executed fake.' Mailer was never one to hold back. In 1971, he headbutted Vidal in the green room a few moments before they both went on the Dick Cavett television show. While no recording of the incident exists, the handbags at dawn that followed on the programme – including a not entirely sober Mailer objecting to being compared to Charles Manson – can be enjoyed online (he also brought up the stabbing of his wife; see p. 18). Half a dozen years later, Mailer belted Gore in the face at a party, to which Vidal in full Oscar Wilde mode retorted, 'Once again, words fail Norman Mailer.' At this stage, Vidal was used to his interlocutors seeing red. Three years earlier, on an ABC television debate, Vidal had called right-wing commentator and novelist William F. Buckley a 'sort of pro or crypto Nazi'. 'Now listen,' replied Buckley, 'stop calling me a crypto-Nazi or I'll sock you in the goddamn face, and you'll stay plastered.'

«5»

# ROMANCE

***Nobody has ever measured, not even poets, how much the heart can hold.***

ZELDA FITZGERALD (ATTRIBUTED)

**Writers have been** caught up in romantic monkey business for thousands of years. But when love breaks down it's not always predictable what the impact will be. Catullus, whose poetry has been a mainstay of Latin lessons for many schoolchildren, found writing inspiration in his affair with Clodia, aka 'Lesbia' (*'vivamus, mea Lesbia, atque amemus'*), wife of either the senator and consul Metellus Celer or Gnaeus Pompeius, elder son of Pompey the Great. Catullus also found heartache when Clodia started seeing his friend Marcus Caelius Rufus. So while this wasn't great for Catullus at the time, it was fabulous for his eternal fame.

Can divorces even help a writer's career? When Dan Brown's marriage to Blythe Brown ended badly in 2019, plenty of details emerged of their relationship, both personal (he had been having an affair with her much younger Dutch horse trainer, to whom he had given a $350,000 Friesian horse called LimiTed) and working. While Dan had always paid tribute to the work Blythe contributed to his bestselling novels, she asserted it was rather more than that, that she'd actually inspired much of his work and indeed come up with the story for *The Da Vinci Code*. But some commentators argued that rather than cast a pall over his career, the media coverage actually may have helped Dan – in an interview with the *Sunday Times*, he reported that when he asked his publisher if it might have an impact on sales, the reply was,'Are you kidding? Everyone thinks you're the most boring guy in the world … multiple affairs with beautiful women, finally there's a story!'

More worrying than an impact on sales is the potential impact of an affair on your life. Sixteenth-century poet Sir Thomas Wyatt knew Anne Boleyn, was said to be an admirer, and there's a case to be made – partly on clues in some of his poems – that their relationship turned romantic. Certainly Anne's husband, Henry VIII, thought so and without any tangible evidence, he banged Wyatt up in the Tower of London for adultery (though he also accused her of an incestuous relationship with her brother, so…).

Wyatt certainly wasn't the last poet to get into trouble. At 4.15 a.m. on 28 July 1814, the twenty-one-year-old Percy Bysshe Shelley eloped with the sixteen-year-old future author of *Frankenstein*, Mary Wollstonecraft Godwin. Leaving his pregnant wife Harriet behind in the lurch, they travelled from London to Paris accompanied by Mary's stepsister Jane. There is even some speculation that Mary lost her virginity to him on the grave of her mother, feminist writer Mary Wollstonecraft, at St Pancras church in London. It's probably impossible to find out the truth, though the couple curiously always referred to that day as his 'birthday'…

Perhaps most famous of all literary love rats was Lord Byron. He met Lady Caroline Lamb for the first time at a dinner party in 1812, a couple of days after seeing her from afar at a soirée when she noted that her immediate impression on seeing him has become one of the most famous descriptions of a likely lad: 'mad – bad – and dangerous to know'. After they met, she invited him to a morning reception at her house the following day and soon afterwards they started a scandalous six-month affair.

Lest there be any doubt about the effect of society's disapproving frown when it comes to romantic entanglements, Oscar Wilde's later life underlines the worst that can happen. Wilde's legal suit against the marquess of Queensberry for criminal libel over his relationship with the marquess's son Lord Alfred 'Bosie' Douglas went horribly wrong. Wilde lost the case, was consequently convicted of gross indecency, went to prison for two years, saw his marriage disintegrate, went into exile in France, and suffered declining health until he died aged just forty-six in 1900.

One way of avoiding public comment when having an affair is simply to keep it quiet. When author of *The Fountainhead* Ayn Rand wanted to have an affair with their mutual friend and her protégé Nathaniel Branden in 1954, she told both her husband Frank and Branden's wife Barbara, and also persuaded them to keep it under their hats. She then told Frank to keep away from their apartment twice a week when Nathaniel would call on her.

As we've already seen (p. 46), Charles Dickens and William Makepeace Thackeray fell out over a throwaway remark by the latter about Dickens's affair with actress Ellen Ternan, which he knew if made public would affect his public profile, not to mention book sales. The liaison certainly ended Dickens's marriage to Catherine, mother of his ten children, and he did not come out of its demise smelling of roses. Instead of an amicable break, Charles went on the offensive, smearing Catherine by suggesting not only that she was a cold, unfit mother (which recently unearthed family letters entirely disprove) but also that she was suffering from mental issues.

He outlined all this in a statement sent to his readings and tour manager Arthur Smith, who then circulated it before it was published in newspapers in the UK and the US. 'For some years past,' wrote the author of *Bleak House*, 'Mrs Dickens has been in the habit of representing to me that it would be better for her to go away and live apart; that her always increasing estrangement made a mental disorder under which she sometimes labours – more, that she felt herself unfit for the life she had to lead as my wife and that she would be better far away.'

Among those who felt he had gone too far was Elizabeth Barrett Browning, who wrote, 'What a dreadful letter that last was! And what a crime, for a man to use his genius as a cudgel against his near kin ... even against the woman he promised to protect tenderly with life & heart – taking advantage of his hold with the public to turn public opinion against her! I call it dreadful.' Dickens then tried to get Catherine incarcerated in a mental asylum, an attempt that failed only because a doctor – probably Dr Thomas Harrington Tuke, superintendent of Manor House Asylum in Chiswick – could find no evidence of the 'mental disorder' Charles claimed.

Dickens was not the only famous writer to try and get his wife institutionalised. One of his good friends was politician and novelist Edward Bulwer-Lytton, perhaps most (in)famous now for the opening lines to his 1830 novel *Paul Clifford*, which begins, 'It was a dark and stormy night.' Bulwer-Lytton and his wife Rosina were not happily married – he was regularly unfaithful and dubbed

'Wifewhack' by *The Age* newspaper – and separated after six years of marriage in 1833. Relations did not improve when in 1858 Rosina heckled him during an election hustings. Bulwer-Lytton responded by preventing her from contacting their children and then having her certified insane and held in an asylum. Released after a couple of weeks, when she was found to be entirely sane and partly thanks to public condemnation of Bulwer-Lytton's actions, she carried on with her criticisms and even wrote the whole sorry story up in her memoir, *A Blighted Life*.

And even though T.S. Eliot's wife Vivienne was only committed to the Northumberland House mental hospital in London in 1938 some years after they had definitively split up, he never visited her there, although she remained his wife.

Some writers, of course, have the best of intentions when they start off life together. Sylvia Plath and Ted Hughes were certainly happy initially as husband and wife, getting married on that most literary of dates, Bloomsday, even if it all went very badly wrong in later years. Leo Tolstoy was very much a believer in honesty being the best policy, so before his marriage to Sophia Behrs on 23 September 1862, he decided to show her his diaries, which catalogued his previous love affairs as well as an illegitimate son he'd fathered with one of his estate serfs. Sophia went ahead with the ceremony but she was certainly not delighted, and in her first diary entry as Mrs Tolstoy on 8 October, she said she was feeling terrible after he told her that he didn't trust her love. 'No sooner am I happy,' she wrote, 'than he crushes me.'

There can be no doubt that the match between poets Elizabeth Barrett and Robert Browning was a love one. It was a respectful but largely secret romance which began in May 1845, the couple keeping things quiet as her authoritarian father regarded Browning as socially below his daughter and a potential gold digger. Consequently, they took advantage of Elizabeth's family's absence on 12 September 1846 to get married at St Marylebone parish church. 'There was no elopement in the case,' she wrote in a letter, 'but simply a private marriage.' She did go home for a week, keeping the wedding a secret, then travelled swiftly with Browning and her dog Flush, and her maid Elizabeth Wilson, to Italy. While it was never a full-blooded social scandal, her father disowned and disinherited her and her brothers shunned her, and she never saw Mr Barrett again, though her sisters were very much on her side. Elizabeth died in June 1861 in Browning's arms.

H.G. Wells looked more like a staid bank manager than a swash-buckling roustabout, but this jokily self-proclaimed '*Don Juan of the Intelligentsia*' had a string of romantic attachments whom he often inserted into his novels only very lightly cloaked. In addition to his wife Catherine, Wells's conquests included his student lover Amy (later his second wife, also known as Jane), novelist Dorothy Richardson, writer Amber Reeves, novelists Elizabeth von Arnim and Rebecca West (who called Wells 'Jaguar' and said 'he frisked like a nice animal'), birth control campaigners Margaret Sanger and Dora Russell (wife of philosopher Bertrand Russell), writer Odette Keun, Maxim Gorky's mistress Moura Budberg, Boston socialite Constance Coolidge, E. Nesbit's daughter the writer Rosamund Bland (whose father prevented her eloping with Wells), literary hostess and novelist Violet Hunt, journalist Hedwig Gatternigg (who attempted suicide in Wells's house) and journalist Martha Gellhorn.

The relationship that caused the most gossip and scandal was the one with Amber Reeves, which began when she was still an undergraduate at Newnham College, Cambridge. Her father William was not at all pleased, and the story goes that he took a pistol to the Savile Club where both he and Wells were members and kept a beady eye out for him, to the extent that the club suggested that to avoid any unpleasantness Wells should resign, which he did, decamping to the Athenaeum for some years. Wells's fellow Fabian Society stalwart Beatrice Webb was among those shocked by his behaviour, writing in her diaries about the 'blackguardism of Wells', his 'total incapacity for decent conduct' and that he 'seduced Amber within the very walls of Newnham, having been permitted, as an old friend, to go to her room'. His friend, the philosopher Bertrand Russell, called him 'an unmitigated cad and scoundrel' in a letter to a friend.

While the pair rented a room near Victoria Station in London to meet up in private, they also seem to have enjoyed sex in multiple locations, including inside a church when pretending to be interested in having a look at the belfry. When she became pregnant, Wells arranged a swift marriage to lawyer George Rivers Blanco White, who was later made King's Counsel. Wells's *roman-à-clef Ann Veronica* was very much based on his relationship with Amber, and his usual publisher Frederick Macmillan in fact turned it down because of its sensational nature. Wells himself was frank about this aspect of his life, writing in his autobiography that 'I was never a great amorist, though I have loved several people very deeply … I have done what I pleased, so that every bit of sexual impulse in me has expressed itself.'

«6»

# CRITICS

*And then to the King's Theatre,*
*where we saw 'Midsummer's Night's Dream',*
*which I had never seen before,*
*nor shall ever again,*
*for it is the most insipid ridiculous play*
*that ever I saw in my life.*

SAMUEL PEPYS, DIARY ENTRY FOR 29 SEPTEMBER 1662

**One of the first** lessons writers must learn is to cope with not merely disappointment but total rejection and withering criticism from publishers and critics (not to mention readers and other writers themselves – 'Writers seldom wish other writers well,' opined novelist Saul Bellow).

Even while the book is still being written, friends can be very cutting. 'Oh God, no more Elves,' was the exasperated comment of English don Professor Hugo Dyson when J.R.R. Tolkien began reading his latest work at one of the meetings of the literary group they were both members of in Oxford, the Inklings. Other reports of his comment suggest what he actually said was the considerably more heartfelt, if somewhat coarse, 'Oh no. Not another fucking elf.'

And in 1926 Ezra Pound wrote a letter to James Joyce about his ongoing attempts to read Joyce's work in progress, which would later become *Finnegans Wake*. 'I will have another go at it,' he promised, 'but up to present I make nothing of it whatever. Nothing so far as I make out, nothing short of divine vision or a new cure for the clapp can possibly be worth all the circumambient peripherization.'

Once the writing is largely done and dusted, a writer's literary agent still has to make the sale. In 1968 Ursula K. Le Guin's representative Virginia Kidd received a rejection letter from an editor at a publishing house who had been sent the manuscript for *The Left Hand of Darkness*. This editor – whose name Le Guin graciously never revealed – did say that she wrote 'extremely well' but was still unable to make an offer. 'The whole is so dry and airless, so lacking in pace, that whatever drama and excitement the novel might have had is entirely dissipated by what does seem, a great deal of the time, to be extraneous material.' *The Wind in the Willows* by Kenneth Grahame was turned down by another publisher on the basis that it was 'an irresponsible holiday story that will never sell'.

Reviews of new books do not always age well, either, such as the verdict of the *New York Times'* book reviewer Orville Prescott on *Lolita* ('dull, dull, dull in a pretentious, florid and archly fatuous fashion') or T.S. Eliot suggesting to George Orwell that *Animal Farm* was too political for Faber to publish ('what was needed, was not more communism but more public-spirited pigs'). 'Stick to your teaching, Miss Alcott,' advised publisher James Fields to the author of *Little Women*. 'You can't write.'

Of course a bad review does not necessarily have any effect on sales. Dorothy Parker's takedown of *The House at Pooh Corner* by A.A. Milne in her 'Constant Reader' column in the *New Yorker* was in her typically caustic style ('And it is that word "hummy", my darlings, that marks the first place in *The House at Pooh Corner* at which Tonstant Weader Fwowed up'), but Milne was the one laughing all the way to the bank. Likewise, Susan Cohen wrote

about Stieg Larsson's *The Girl With the Dragon Tattoo* in the *Charleston City Paper* that 'this is easily one of the worst books I've ever read. And bear in mind that I've read John Grisham.' It was not a career-ender for either writer. 'It is advantageous to an author that his book should be attacked as well as praised,' proclaimed Dr Samuel Johnson. 'Fame is a shuttlecock. If it be struck at only one end of the room, it will soon fall to the ground. To keep it up, it must be struck at both ends.'

However, it should be remembered that book reviewing can be a demanding calling too. In George Orwell's essay '*Confessions of a Book Reviewer*', he argues that 'the prolonged, indiscriminate reviewing of books is a quite exceptionally thankless, irritating and exhausting job' and that the poor melancholy book reviewer is 'pouring his immortal spirit down the drain, half a pint at a time'. Orwell was a prolific reviewer, getting through more than 700 appraisals in 20 years on the job, 135 of which were in 1940 alone. That's a lot of pints.

Sometimes reviews can also be tinged with danger, since not all writers take criticism stoically. After reading Alice Hoffman's appraisal of his novel *The Sportswriter* in the *New York Times*, author Richard Ford (not notable for shrugging his shoulders in the face of criticism, as we've already seen) grabbed a gun and shot one of Hoffman's own novels. Apparently Ford's wife also contributed a bullet to its destruction. Ford then posted it to Hoffman in bits – which seems particularly severe since the review was not that bad at all, including for example her view that it showed 'an extraordinary ear for dialogue and the ability to create the particulars of everyday life with stunning accuracy'.

At the end of the day, is it worth the energy? 'I have long felt that any reviewer who expresses rage and loathing for a novel is preposterous,' said Kurt Vonnegut in his miscellaneous collection *Palm Sunday: An Autobiographical Collage*. 'He or she is like a person who has put on full armor and attacked a hot fudge sundae or a banana split.'

Here is an alphabetical tour of contemporaries' hot takes:

## A is for *American Psycho*

Poet laureate Sir Andrew Motion did not mince his words when reviewing Bret Easton Ellis's disturbing novel for the *Observer* in 1991, calling it not only 'numbingly boring' throughout but also 'for much of the time deeply and extremely disgusting. Not interesting-disgusting, but disgusting-disgusting.' Motion added that it was merely a vehicle for making money and becoming a sensation.

## B is for Brontë

Emily Brontë kept reviews of her books in her writing desk, and while she never left us her thoughts about them, she can hardly have been delighted with the reception *Wuthering Heights* was given by the critics.

'There is an old saying that those who eat toasted cheese at night will dream of Lucifer,' said the anonymous reviewer in the Philadelphia-based *Graham's Lady's Magazine* in 1848, a year after it was first published. 'The author of *Wuthering Heights* has evidently eaten toasted cheese. How a human being could have attempted such a book as the present without committing suicide before he had finished a dozen chapters, is a mystery. It is a compound of vulgar depravity and unnatural horrors.'

At least, James Lorimer comforted himself in the 1847 *North British Review*, 'the only consolation which we have in reflecting upon it is that it will never be generally read'.

## C is for *Catch-22*

Joseph Heller's war novel 'gasps for want of craft and sensibility', said Richard G. Stern in 1961 in the pages of the *New York Times Book Review*, or to put it another way, the book was 'an emotional hodgepodge'. The *New Yorker* the same year was equally unimpressed. 'It doesn't even seem to be written. Instead, it gives the impression of having been shouted on to paper.'

## D is for Charles Dickens

Writing in 1839 in the *Quarterly Review*, travel writer and wealthy son-in-law of the Earl of Essex Richard Ford had several problems with *Oliver Twist*. First of all, he argues boldly: 'The abuses which he [Dickens] ridicules are not only exaggerated, but in nineteen cases out of twenty do not at all exist.' Moreover, Ford pointed to the plot's many improbabilities and Oliver's angelic innocence and suggested that 'less absurd would it be to expect to gather grapes on thorns, to find pearls on dunghills, violets in Drury Lane, or make silk purses of sows' ears'.

Other critics had some similarly negative opinions about Dickens's other works, such as *Bleak House* ('More than any of its predecessors it is chargeable with not simply faults, but absolute want of construction', George Brimley, *Spectator*, 1853) and *Our*

*Mutual Friend* ('the greatest of superficial novelists', novelist Henry James, *The Nation*, 1865).

### E is for George Eliot

Here's Henry James being sniffy again, this time in *The Galaxy: A Magazine of Entertaining Reading* in 1873. '*Middlemarch* is a treasure-house of details, but it is an indifferent whole.'

### F is for F. Scott Fitzgerald

'Mr Scott Fitzgerald deserves a good shaking,' said L.P. Hartley in the *Saturday Review* in 1926, a view probably shared by many people. 'Here is an unmistakable talent unashamed of making itself a motley to the view. *The Great Gatsby* is an absurd story, whether considered as romance, melodrama, or plain record of New York high life.' Or to put it another way, the novel was 'obviously unimportant ... no more than a glorified anecdote' (H.L. Mencken, *Chicago Tribune*, 1925) and 'falls into the class of negligible novels' (anoymous reviewer in the *Springfield Republican*, also 1925). And like Dickens, his detractors pounced on others in his catalogue. When *Tender Is the Night* came out nearly a decade later, J. Donald Adams regretfully notified readers of the *New York Times* that 'Bad news is best blurted out at once: "Tender Is the Night" is a disappointment.'

### G is for William Golding

Reviewers in 1954 were often in two minds when it came to Golding's masterpiece *Lord of the Flies*. The author cannot have been wholly delighted with the *New York Times* comment that 'if criticism must be leveled at such a feat of the imagination, it is permissible to carp at the very premise on which the whole strange story is founded', or the *New Yorker*'s 'well-written but completely unpleasant story' or even the *New York Herald Tribune*'s mixed 'too many nagging questions remain unanswered, but the magic of a born story-teller makes us forget our reservations.'

## H is for *The Handmaid's Tale*

For Mary McCarthy, reviewing Margaret Atwood's tale of patriarchal dystopia in the *New York Times* in 1986, there was one standout issue: 'The most conspicuous lack, in comparison with the classics of the fearsome-future genre, is the inability to imagine a language to match the changed face of common life.' For McCarthy, this was 'a serious defect, unpardonable maybe for the genre: a future that has no language invented for it lacks a personality. That must be why, collectively, it is powerless to scare.'

## I is for Laura Ingalls Wilder

The power of a critical review in 2000 by Frances W. Kaye in *Great Plains Quarterly* had a huge effect on the legacy of Laura '*Little House on the Prairie*' Ingalls Wilder. Her article 'Little Squatter on the Osage Diminished Reserve: Reading Laura Ingalls Wilder's Kansas Indians' revealed Kaye was not a fan of the hugely popular book series. 'I honestly cannot read *Little House on the Prairie* as other than apology for the "ethnic cleansing" of the Great Plains,' she said. When, some years later, the American Library Association resolved to drop Laura Ingalls Wilder's name from its children's literature award and change it to the Children's Literature Legacy Award, it cited Kaye's piece as part of its decision-making process.

### J is for *Jazz*

'Bedazzled by her own virtuosity' was novelist Edna O'Brien's 1992 view in the *New York Times* of Toni Morison's novel *Jazz*.

### K is for Jack Kerouac

On 5 September 1957, Gilbert Millstein gave Kerouac's *On the Road* a hearty thumbs up in his *New York Times* review. But the fickle finger of literary fate pointed the other way three days later when David Dempsey, for the same august organ, pronounced it only a 'passionate lark.' There was good and bad in it, suggested Ben Ray Redman of the *Chicago Tribune*. 'He can slip from magniloquent hysteria into sentimental bathos, and at his worst he merely slobbers words.' Kerouac was also among the Beat Generation writers whose works Truman Capote described memorably and disapprovingly on various occasions (and in slightly different wordings) as typing, not writing.

### L is for *Leaves of Grass*

Canny self-promoter Walt Whitman was happy to cut out the middleman, reviewing his own book anonymously in 1855 in the *United States Review*, the *American Phrenological Journal* and the *Brooklyn Daily Eagle*. 'An American bard at last!' he wrote humbly of *Leaves of Grass*. 'With light and rapid touch he first indicates in prose the principles of the foundation of a race of poets.'

Less enthusiastic was the *London Critic* that year. 'Whitman is as unacquainted with art as a hog is with mathematics.' Calvin Beach in June 1860 in the *New York Saturday Press* went some distance further. 'I doubt if, when Judgment-Day comes,' he wrote, 'Walt Whitman's name will be called. He certainly has not enough soul to be saved.' Then he makes the inexplicably cruel suggestion that Whitman make an act of reparation for writing the book by committing suicide: 'Let him search the coast of his island home until he finds some cove where the waves are accustomed to cast up the carrion committed to them, and where their bloated bodies ride lazily upon the waters which humanity never disturbs, and casting himself therein find at last the companionship for which, in death as in life, he is best fitted.' Though Calvin wrote the review, he actually signed it using his wife Juliette's name, which the newspaper used. Juliette herself said she liked *Leaves of Grass*.

## M is for Herman Melville and *Moby-Dick*

*Moby-Dick* rather befuddled many of its early reviewers on publication in 1851: they found both good and puzzling elements in its pages. Henry F. Chorley in the pages of the *London Athenaeum* on 25 October 1851 found it 'a most provoking book' but less approvingly also suggested it was 'so much trash belonging to the worst school of Bedlam literature'. Trying to get his head around the book's various elements, William Young in the *New York Albion* in the same year offered this appraisal: 'It is having oil, mustard, vinegar, and pepper served up as a dish, in place of being scientifically administered sauce-wise.' The anonymous reviewer in the

*London Literary Gazette* felt it was 'wantonly eccentric; outrageously bombastic' and that the detailed whale lore Melville included served 'only to try the patience of his readers, and to tempt them to wish both him and his whales at the bottom of an unfathomable sea'. The unsigned review in the *New York United States Magazine and Democratic Review* the following January, however, was definitely not undecided. 'If there are any of our readers who wish to find examples of bad rhetoric, involved syntax, stilted sentiment and incoherent English, we will take the liberty of recommending to them this precious volume of Mr Melville's.'

### N is for *The Naked and the Dead* and Norman Mailer

Extremely popular and an immediate bestseller on its publication in 1948, Mailer's Second World War novel did not strike a chord with the *New Republic*'s reviewer, who called it 'a transcription of soldiers' talk, lusterless griping and ironed-out obscenities, too detailed and monotonous to have been imaginatively conceived for any larger purpose'. Across the pond, the following year saw the *Daily Telegraph* proclaim it 'dull' and the *Times Literary Supplement* 'increasingly unreadable'.

### O is for *Of Mice and Men*

'A fairy tale … an oxymoronic combination of the tough and tender, *Of Mice And Men* will appeal to sentimental cynics, cynical sentimentalists,' said *Time* magazine's March 1937 reviewer of John Steinbeck's novella, which regularly appears on lists of the most banned or challenged books. 'Readers less easily thrown off their trolley will still prefer Hans Andersen.'

## P is for *Portnoy's Complaint* and Philip Roth

'The cruelest thing anyone can do with *Portnoy's Complaint* is to read it twice ... brief as it is, the book seems half again too long.' Irving Howe in the monthly magazine *Commentary* in 1972, three years after the book came out.

## Q is for *A Question of Upbringing*

The first volume in Anthony Powell's *roman fleuve* running to a dozen separate novels in his *A Dance to the Music of Time* series did not hit the spot for Lucretia Cole in the *Los Angeles Daily News* of 25 August 1951. 'This, I think, is the kind of English novel which drives susceptible American readers to the snug and erroneous conclusion that all English novels are affected, snail-paced and glum. It is impossible to convey in mere words the tedium of Anthony Powell's prose.'

## R is for J.K. Rowling

Rather than focus on a single title, the *Observer* columnist Anthony Holden took the whole *Harry Potter* series to task in a full-blown takedown in 2000 which drew quite the postbag the following week. While he wished Joanne Rowling good luck ('I warm to the modest way in which she appears to have handled her huge success'), he also argued: 'As a workout for the brain, reading (or being read) *Harry Potter* is an activity marginally less testing than watching *Neighbours* ... These are one-dimensional children's books, Disney cartoons written in words, no more ... a tedious, clunkily written version of Billy Bunter on broomsticks ... patronising, very conservative, highly derivative, dispiritingly nostalgic for a bygone Britain which only ever existed at Greyfriars and St Trinian's.'

### S is for *The Sun Also Rises*

No matter what the critics said about Ernest Hemingway's debut novel, the most important person in his life was definitely not keen. When fellow members of her book club told her in no uncertain terms that they thought Ernest had not produced his best work, Grace wrote a letter to her son (which he kept), saying: 'It is a doubtful honor to produce one of the filthiest books of the year … What is the matter? Have you ceased to be interested in nobility, honor and fineness in life? … Surely you have other words in your vocabulary than "damn" and "bitch". Every page fills me with a sick loathing.' Thanks mum.

### T is for Mark Twain

As controversial when it was published in 1884 as it is now, Twain's *Adventures of Huckleberry Finn* was not on the *Springfield Republican*'s Books of the Year list. The paper called it 'trashy and vicious … no better in tone than the dime novels which flood the blood-and-thunder reading population'.

### U is for *Ulysses*

'Appears written by a perverted lunatic who has made a speciality of the literature of the latrine … Two-thirds of it is incoherent, and the passages that are plainly written are devoid of wit,' growled the *Sporting Times* about James Joyce's modernist day-long novel in 1922. Or as the ever classist Virginia Woolf said in her diary, 'An illiterate, underbred book it seems to me: the book of a self-taught working man, and we all know how distressing they are, how egotistic, insistent, raw, striking, and ultimately nauseating.'

## V is for Vonnegut

Kurt Vonnegut was nothing if not self-critical. 'You understand, of course,' he told his interviewer David Standish in a piece for *Playboy* in 1973, 'that everything I say is horseshit.' Jack Richardson, reviewing his 1969 war novel *Slaughterhouse Five* in the *New York Review of Books*, appeared to agree, arguing 'when all of its wearisome inventiveness is done, [it is] one of the most unsurprising, self-indulgent little books ever to work so hard at being selfless and memorable'. Vonnegut also kept the many rejection slips he received from magazines to which he had offered his short stories, framing and hanging some of them, while the rest were upcycled by his wife Jane to decorate a waste basket.

## W is for *Where the Wild Things Are*

'The plan and technique of the illustrations are superb,' proclaimed *Publishers Weekly* when Maurice Sendak's children's story about anger diffusion came out, before qualifying it with 'but they may well prove frightening, accompanied as they are by a pointless and confusing story.' Or as the *Cleveland Press* said with a wink: 'Boys and girls may have to shield their parents from this book. Parents are very easily scared.'

## X is for Xavier Herbert

Australian writer Herbert – who disliked semicolons so much he wrenched the key off his typewriter – is best known for his enormous 1975 book *Poor Fellow My Country*, which weighs in at 1,463 pages, making it the longest Australian novel. The *Nation Review* commented, 'poor fellow Xavier Herbert's typewriter' (which is a reminder of *Newsweek* reviewer Jack Beatty's comment on James A. Michener's 865-page *Chesapeake* – 'My best advice is don't read it: my second best is don't drop it on your foot.')

### Y is for W.B. Yeats

'Yeats's drama shares many of the same obsessions and even much of the linguistic beauty of his poetry, but his self-conscious, humourless aesthetic smothers the delicate emotion and lightness.' Chris Moran, *Guardian*, 24 April 2009, seemingly not a fan.

### Z is for Zafón

And finally, here's Jennie Yabroff from the *San Francisco Chronicle*, who appeared to find *The Shadow of the Wind* by Carlos Ruiz Zafón heavy going. 'The combined effect of the foggy setting and soggy writing is of being lost in a swamp … Soon enough the mists blow back in, though, and the flame under this tepid potboiler goes out for good.'

Ever resourceful, writers have various ways of getting their own back. 'The first agent I ever queried sent back a slip saying, "My list is full. The folder you sent wouldn't fit in the envelope,"' tweeted J.K. Rowling in 2015, adding playfully: 'I now have over a million folders, all made of costly silks, each one hand-gilded by artisans in Paris.' And E.E. Cummings dedicated his self-published *No Thanks* collection to the fourteen publishers who turned it down, arranging their names in the shape of a funeral urn.

# Part II: BOOKS

«7»

# ENDINGS

*Boys, however, are by far more destructive than girls, and have, naturally, no reverence for age, whether in man or books.*

*THE ENEMIES OF BOOKS*, WILLIAM BLADES

**Books are constantly** in danger. In 1888, William Blades published his short volume *The Enemies of Books*, in which he focused on the many and varied ways they can bite the dust. Over ten chapters he pointed an accusatory finger at fire, water, neglect, gas and heat, ignorance and bigotry, the bookworm and other vermin, bookbinders, collectors, servants and children. There was one book killer, though, that Blades picked out for special mention. 'There are many of the forces of Nature which tend to injure books,' he wrote, 'but among them all not one has been half so destructive as fire.'

Fire is a particularly brutal destroyer of words, which has given rise to one of the most famous undertakings asked of readers, the Bodleian Library's declaration:

> *Do fidem me nullum librum vel instrumentum aliamve quam rem ad bibliothecam pertinentem, vel ibi custodiae causa depositam, aut e bibliotheca sublaturum esse, aut foedaturum deformaturum aliove quo modo laesurum; item neque ignem nec flammam in bibliothecam inlaturum vel in ea accensurum,*

> *neque fumo nicotiano aliove quovis ibi usurum; item promitto me omnes leges ad bibliothecam Bodleianam attinentes semper observaturum esse.*

Students now repeat this in English (or in their mother tongue, as it has been translated into more than 100 languages):

> *I hereby undertake not to remove from the Library, or to mark, deface, or injure in any way, any volume, document, or other object belonging to it or in its custody; not to bring into the Library or kindle therein any fire or flame, and not to smoke in the Library; and I promise to obey all rules of the Library.*

As an example of what damage fire can do, look no further than manuscript collector Sir Robert Cotton, who did the country a great service in bringing together unique written treasures including two original Magna Cartas, a manuscript of *Sir Gawain and the Green Knight*, and the Lindisfarne Gospels, which astoundingly survived the clutches of the eighth-century rampaging Vikings.

Unfortunately, it was a case of one basket and all your eggs when Ashburnham House in Westminster, where these and many other items were all kept, was devastated by fire in October 1731. Asser's *Life of Alfred* perished, as did *The Battle of Maldon*, while the vellum copy of *Beowulf* (now in safer conditions at the British Library) got a bit blistered. The immediate report of damage sent to a specially set-up parliamentary committee suggested 114 volumes were lost, burnt or 'intirely spoiled', though thanks to fine restoration work the final total of absolute losses is nearer the dozen mark.

Fire continues to be an insatiable enemy. The Theosophical Society buildings in Altadena near Pasadena were completely destroyed in the 2025 Los Angeles fires. Among them was the society's archive and library, home to around 40,000 titles and 10,000 unpublished letters which amounted to the world's largest collection of materials about the modern religious movement among whose adherents was poet W.B. Yeats.

Sometimes works are deliberately thrown onto the fire. Gung-ho British troops burnt down the first Library of Congress in 1814 as they went on the rampage in Washington, DC; more systematically, the Nazis turned thousands of volumes into ash between 1933 and 1945. But authors themselves sometimes prefer fiery annihilation to the back of the drawer. James Joyce threw his manuscript of *Stephen Hero*, an early version of what would become *A Portrait of the Artist*, into the flames, and it was thanks to his quick-thinking sister Eileen – or, as Joyce described her, the 'family fire-brigade', who yanked it out again – that any of it survives. Nikolai Gogol went even further, burning the second section of his planned three-volume novel *Dead Souls* twice, first in 1845 and then the rewritten manuscript in 1852, though it's not clear exactly whether he simply thought it was no good or it was a very unfortunate accident.

'Yesterday I burnt, in the field at Gad's Hill, the accumulated letters and papers of twenty years,' Charles Dickens wrote to a friend in September 1860. 'They set up a smoke like the genie when he got out of the casket on the seashore; and as it was an exquisite day when I began, and rained very heavily when I finished, I suspect my correspondence of having overcast the face of the heavens.' Four years later he explained in another letter that, 'shocked by the misuse of private letters of public men, which I constantly observed, I destroyed a very large and very rare mass of correspondence. It was not done without pain, you may believe, but, the first reluctance, conquered, I have steadily abided by my determination to keep no letters by me, and to consign all such papers to the fire.'

American novelist Henry James also burnt decades of correspondence in his old age, though Philip Larkin was among those who changed their minds about a fiery spring clean. He told his fellow poet – later to become his biographer – Andrew Motion that when he felt he was nearing death he would burn everything he did not want anybody to read. He failed to do this, but his instructions to get rid of his diaries were faithfully carried out by his secretary and lover Betty Mackereth, who dutifully whizzed them through a paper shredder.

V. S. Naipaul certainly had no hand in the destruction of much of his early writings. In the 1970s he put the manuscript of his first novel, *The Shadow'd Livery*, into a storage facility in London along with many of his letters and diaries and other assorted book manuscripts. Sadly, when he came to take a look at them two decades later, it turned out they had been reduced to ashes when the company had mistakenly included all boxes marked 'Naipaul' in a clear-out of all boxes marked 'Nitrate'.

There is no doubt at all about the extremely deliberate burning in 1824 of Lord Byron's memoirs, diaries and correspondence written between 1818 and 1821. His publisher, John Murray, alongside half a dozen of Byron's friends, decided to incinerate them at Murray's London offices in Albemarle Street because they were so indecent. 'When you read my Memoirs you will learn the evils, moral and physical, of true dissipation,' trumpeted Byron. 'I can assure you my life is very entertaining and very instructive.' How indecent they were we will never know, even though copies had already appeared in the wild at the time that they were burnt and were read by Percy and Mary Shelley, as well as Byron's lover Lady Caroline Lamb.

There is of course a strand of book burning which veers into the realms of censorship, stretching back thousands of years. To take one example, when D.H. Lawrence published his sexually controversial novel *The Rainbow* in September 1915, it received pretty hostile reviews before the authorities sent in the police, who seized at least 1,000 copies of the book from publishers Methuen and printers Hazell, Watson and Viney. After a successful prosecution under the Obscene Publications Act 1857, the books were burnt outside the Royal Exchange in London by a hangman (which feels like overkill) and the novel was banned for another decade. Of course, it is very hard to really eradicate books, and first editions continue to crop up in antiquarian booksellers' catalogues today.

In the digital age, it is regarded as bad form to burn your backups. As he approached his death in 2015, Terry Pratchett wanted to be absolutely sure that nobody was going to fool around with the works he had in progress after he had gone. So in his will he stipulated that his hard drive should be obliterated by a steamroller after he had gone. This was carried out as ordered, and ten partially finished novels met Death's scythe.

Sometimes though the flames can provide inspiration. When a fire destroyed fifty-one-year-old playwright Ben Jonson's personal library and various works in progress in 1623, he took to his quill and described the conflagration in a 200-line disaster poem entitled 'An Execration upon Vulcan'. Overall, he took it all surprisingly well. So did Thomas Carlyle when his friend John Stuart Mill visited him at his London home in March 1834 in a state of panic. Carlyle had lent him a copy of his current work in progress, a history of the French Revolution. Mill had then passed it on to a friend, whose maid accidentally used the whole manuscript to light a fire. The stoical Carlyle simply rewrote it, though he was slightly hampered by having himself binned all his notes.

There are countless ways to lose a manuscript. During downtime at your job, you write a novel and in a moment of madness accidentally leave it in a pram and it is lost forever. It could happen to any of us. In this case, poor Miss Prism's work, which Lady Bracknell describes harshly in *The Importance of Being Earnest* as 'a three-volume novel of more than usually

revolting sentimentality', is never heard of again once it is mentioned. Its fate is certainly not unique: there are many real-world examples of valuable texts going astray – in a railway station café (where T.E. Lawrence left a draft of *Seven Pillars of Wisdom* in Reading), on a number 22 bus in London (Jilly Cooper and her copy of *Riders*), from your publisher's open-top sports car (Malcolm Lowry's first novel, *Ultramarine*), on the train between Newcastle and Durham (J.M. Falkner's unnamed fourth novel), and on a boozy shore leave in San Francisco (Robert Ludlum's first novel, written when he was a US Marine). The classic schoolboy excuse for homework absence, 'the dog ate it', summed up a wretched real-life disaster for John Steinbeck, whose spaniel Toby gulped down most of the first draft of *Of Mice and Men* in 1936. Remarkably, a scrap of this turned up at auction at Sotheby's in 2023 and sold for $12,800. It read: '… *George*." Lenny's hands went … had it. I got both of 'em here … What you got in your hand …' on one side, and on the reverse '… bank the dead … noise shattering an … evening. The lambs … from the rear.' Only one other fragment

is believed to have survived Toby's jaws, and that is badly chewed.

You'd hope that you could trust the very people who have your best interests at heart to look after your work properly and yet … L. Frank Baum of *Wizard of Oz* fame appears to have written four novels that have never been found in manuscript form and are only known about through Baum's notes, *Johnson* (1912), *Our Married Life* (1912), *The Mystery of Bonita* (1914) and *Molly Oodle* (1915). His publishers Reilly & Britton even had copies of *Johnson* and *Molly Oodle* at some point but simply failed to hang on to them.

There are plenty of scary near-miss tales which should keep twenty-first-century writers on their backup toes. Dylan Thomas (whom we have met before and will meet again, it's his sort of a book) claimed that he lost the first manuscript of *Under Milk Wood* on a trip to Cardiff, where it turned up in his suitcase at his hotel, and another in London, where it somewhat inevitably was found at a pub in Soho (it's not entirely clear if it was the French House or Helvetia), where the barmaid had kept it nice and safe under the counter.

Charles Dickens nearly lost the section of *Our Mutual Friend* he was working on in the horrific Stapleton train crash in June 1865 in which ten people died. When Dickens was returning from a holiday in France with Ellen Ternan, his mistress, the train derailed near Maidstone. Although he later suffered some sort of post-traumatic stress disorder, Dickens was physically unhurt and nobly did what he could to help the injured and other survivors. When the rescue teams arrived, he only remembered to retrieve his manuscript at the last moment from his overcoat pocket in his train carriage.

Water can also be a dangerous playmate for books. When RMS *Titanic* hit an iceberg on its maiden voyage from Southampton to New York, among the volumes that went down with the ship were a magnificent 1911 *Rubaiyat of Omar Khayyam* known as 'The Great Omar' for its gold leaf and binding by Sangorski & Sutcliffe featuring three golden peacocks with jewelled tails, a 1598 edition of Sir Francis Bacon's *Essays*, and probably the original illustrations for *The Mystery of Edwin Drood*, the novel left unfinished by Dickens when he died.

While natural disasters claim many books, so do light-fingered burglars. A short *Harry Potter* prequel written by J.K. Rowling on an A5 postcard and sold for £25,000 at a Waterstones charity auction in 2008 was pinched in Birmingham in 2017. It has not yet come to light. In terms of the most stolen titles from bookshops, this obviously changes over time. Terry Pratchett's oeuvre was leading the way in the UK in the mid-1990s (science fiction and fantasy is a perennial favourite section, as is – maybe surprisingly – philosophy) at a time when Charles Bukowski's was doing the same in New York. A decade later, and before mobile phones ruined its market share, the London A–Z was the most popular shoplifted book in the capital, with Tolkien and *Harry Potter* hard on its heels.

Joe Orton and his lover Kenneth Halliwell were found guilty of theft and malicious damages for a three-year campaign in the late 1950s and early 1960s during which they defaced dozens of books in Islington Public Library. Shakespeare's plays and Agatha Christie novels were particular targets, and on the flyleaf of *Clouds of Witness* by Dorothy L. Sayers the duo added an amended précis that suggested it focused on child abuse and ended with the advice to library users to 'Read this behind closed doors! And have a good shit while you are reading!' They also pinched plates from art books and turned them into an impressive collage in their London flat.

Not all authors dislike their books being half-inched – Irvine Welsh, author of *Trainspotting*, which itself features book theft prominently, once said he rather appreciated people stealing it from bookshops as it meant he got a guaranteed royalty as a result. In an anecdotal survey by the *Guardian* newspaper in 2017, Blackwells in Oxford also noted that any books on the GCSE and A Level reading lists were always going missing. When it comes to the record for books disappearing from public libraries, according to *The Guinness Book of Records* (now called *Guinness World Records*) the holder is *The Guinness Book of Records*.

Making it a little harder for the more expensive titles that vanish to be resold is the book register launched in 2021 by the International League of Antiquarian Booksellers, who generously only call it a 'Missing Books Register'. Even when all seems lost, some of these iconic books still make it back home. Two of Charles Darwin's personal notebooks containing his famous 1837 'Tree of Life' sketch went walkabout from Cambridge University Library sometime around the year 2000, and after twenty years of searching they were officially announced as stolen in 2020. After a public appeal this cornerstone of scientific endeavour turned up safe and sound in 2022 in a manila envelope inside a pink gift bag with a note wishing the library a Happy Easter.

It is certainly good news when that which is lost is found. James Michener finished his novel *Hawaii* and then weighed up whether Mexico or Scotland should be the setting for his next epic. Eventually settling for the former, with a central bullfighting theme, he had pretty much finished it three years later when he sadly misplaced it. He recounted what happened to it in his 1993 account, *My Lost Mexico: The Making of a Novel,* in which he explained that when his Random House editor Bennett Cerf offered some criticism (any reason it featured a Hollywood couple suspiciously like Janet Leigh and Tony Curtis? he asked), he took it very much to heart and simply stopped working on it. He then sent it lock, stock and barrel to the Library of Congress for safe keeping, where it promptly disappeared for thirty years until it turned up in a couple of cardboard boxes.

Also on the missing list were Walt Whitman's notebooks, which were re-archived around 1942 from their normal home in the Library of Congress in Washington to a nameless library in the Midwest for safekeeping during the war. But when they were eventually unpacked, ten had somehow gone astray, along with a large cardboard butterfly, even though the packing case seals were intact. Fast forward fifty years to 1995, when four of them, including early drafts of 'Song of Myself' (plus the butterfly), turned up at Sotheby's with somebody claiming they had been gifted to his father decades earlier. Everybody involved did the right thing and they were handed back to the Library of Congress. Which leaves six still out in the wild, and archivists are optimistic they could still find their way home some day.

Of course, sometimes it's a blessing that a manuscript has gone the way of all flesh. Sir Arthur Conan Doyle's first novel, the catchily titled *Narrative of John Smith,* was lost in the post on its way to a potential publisher and has never been found. Despite this setback, things turned out ok for this young writer and he admitted in an article for *The Idler* magazine that 'my shock at its disappearance would be as nothing to my horror if it were suddenly to appear again – in print'. Unfortunately for him, it kind of did, since he rewrote it from memory and it languished among his papers after his death before being published finally in 2011, to quite mixed reviews.

Even less likely to turn up is the first manuscript of *1066 and All That* by W. C. Sellar and R. J. Yeatman, which they claim in the preface was printed on rice paper but then left by one of them 'in a taxi somewhere between Piccadilly Circus and the Bodleian'. And definitely not coming back are the 2,500,000 pulped Mills & Boon novels whose fabulous absorbent qualities were key in the making of the asphalt currently in operation as the M6. A spokesman for the Tarmac company which carried out the procedure was at pains to emphasise that it did not represent a slight on the novels' literary value since 'other books are down there too'.

Of course one problem is that we don't know exactly what we don't have any more. Like much ancient Greek and Roman literature for which we know only the titles, Aristotle's work on humour doesn't seem to have made it to the present day, other than via a MacGuffin-ish appearance in Umberto Eco's novel *The Name of the Rose*. The dissolution of the monasteries in the sixteenth century was responsible for the plentiful destruction of who knows what – William Blades shook his head at the results, in which 'the paper books with all their artistic ornaments went to the bakers to heat their ovens, and the parchment manuscripts, however beautifully illuminated, to the binders and boot makers.' Indeed, one 2022 study suggested that a figure somewhere north of 90 per cent of manuscripts produced in medieval Europe have simply not survived to the twenty-first century.

My
Secrete
Long Lost
Extremely
Valuable
Boke

«8»

# FAKE

*The secret of success is sincerity.*
*Once you can fake that you've got it made.*

ATTRIBUTED TO GROUCHO MARX. AND GEORGE BURNS.
AND SAMUEL GOLDWYN. AND LEONARD LYONS.

**Just because authorship** isn't entirely clear cut doesn't mean somebody is pulling a fast one. It's generally accepted that Laura Ingalls Wilder's daugher Rose Wilder Lane helped her mother to some degree with the *Little House on the Prairie* series; the only area for discussion is exactly how much – somewhere between mild copyediting and complete rewrites, depending on who you believe.

Yet it's true that fraudulent literary production has a long and ignoble history. Snippets of Cicero's philosophical book about consolation have survived, but these were not enough for sixteenth-century Italian scholar Carlo Sigonius, who claimed he had managed to lay his hands on the full manuscript in 1583. He had, of course, done no such thing. Nor, nearly 200 years later in 1761, had James Macpherson come across and then translated a cycle of poems by the forgotten third-century Celtic bard Ossian about Fionn mac Cumhaill/Finn McCool, for the simple reason that Ossian did not exist. More recently, poems published in literary magazines in the 1990s by Araki Yasusada, a Hiroshima bomb survivor, were real enough but Yasusada himself was not.

Satirical American writer Kent Johnson was probably the power behind the poet, though he consistently denied it.

Two of the most intriguing names in literary forgery were Constantine Simonides and Thomas James Wise. Wise (1859–1937) was a bona fide collector of seventeenth- to nineteenth-century literature turned forger, who became President of the Bibliographical Society. He became known for his astounding ability to root out first editions; he named his famous personal collection the Ashley Library after the London road he lived in. But despite a very real bibliographic skill, he had also turned to the dark side. In an impressively creative effort he printed around 300 forged works, including rare 'first editions' such as a previously unheard of first printing of *Sonnets from the Portuguese* by Elizabeth Barrett Browning. These even found their way into the British Library catalogue. His fertile criminal imagination also came out with the marvellous scam of interleaving genuine pages from other manuscripts which he'd pinched from the British Museum into the copies he produced to add an authentic touch.

Partly because he seemed to be 'discovering' so many remarkable finds, he was eventually found out and exposed, towards the end of his life, by two amateur sleuthing young booksellers. John W. Carter and Henry Graham Pollard used new forensic techniques of paper and ink analysis as well as concentrating on the age of typefaces used by Wise to flush him out. In an ironic turn of events, the Ashley Library – which does actually consist of many valuable literary manuscripts – is now part of the holdings of the British Library.

Operational at around the same time, Simonides (1820–1867) was a Greek antiques and book dealer. But as well as straightforward ancient manuscript forgeries, including a barely believable example of what appeared to be a remarkably early – and naturally unheard of – copy of the first three books of Homer's *Iliad*, he then went on to claim that he had in his teens forged something he hadn't, the entirely genuine fourth-century Codex Sinaiticus copy of the Bible.

You can't fool all of the people all of the time, but East German forger Konrad Kujau made an impressive attempt in the early 1980s when he amazingly 'discovered' sixty previously unseen diaries written by Adolf Hitler which – cue Ring of Truth klaxon – had been recovered from a plane crash and then hidden in a barn for decades. On the basis of in for a penny in for a pound, Kujau said that in addition to the journals he was also in possession of the original manuscript for the unpublished third volume of *Mein Kampf*, an opera written by Hitler as a young man called *Wieland der Schmied* (*Wayland the Smith*), plus plenty of letters and unpublished papers. Titbits from the diaries included the Führer's thoughts on Eva Braun's puppies, positive views on Stalin's purges, and Adolf's own troubling issue with flatulence. Among those who were taken in were German magazine *Stern* (which bought them for millions of pounds) and leading academic Hugh Trevor-Roper (who then changed his mind).

Diaries are a popular arena for forgers. Discovered 400 years after he sailed the ocean blue, the superbly titled 'My Secrete Log Boke', a lost diary written in English by Christopher Columbus from the fifteenth century, was thrown by him from the *Nina Pinta* in a lead-lined casket, then drifted to the Pembroke coast of Wales, where it was found and handed down within a family until it was published in 1892 by Frz. Rangette & Sons of Düsseldorf.

To add extra layers of authenticity for you sceptical unbelievers, the cover shows some water damage as well as traces of seaweed and shells. It was apparently offered to the British Library several times in the first half of the twentieth century. Party poopers the New Zealand National Library attribute what is one of the most popular literary hoaxes to satirical nineteenth-century painter and writer Karl Maria Seyppel, and indeed identical copies in German also exist.

Far less jovial is the case of *The Education of Little Tree*, an autobiographical story published in 1976 by Forrest Carter about his upbringing as a Cherokee lad living with his grandparents. The book was actually written by Asa Earl Carter, not a Cherokee at all but a white segregationist and Ku Klux Klan member from Alabama, as well as the author of the novel on which Clint Eastwood's film *The Outlaw Josey Wales* was based.

He's not the only one who has been economical with the truth. When Howard Hughes's autobiography was sold in 1971 to McGraw-Hill for around $750,000 and the serial rights went to *Life* magazine, it was news to him since he had written no such thing. Step forward writers Clifford Irving and Richard Suskind who had come up with the entire scam, done plenty of research into the extremely reclusive film and aviation mogul Hughes's life, and then invented the rest on the basis that Hughes valued his privacy so much he would not break cover. Initially the pair claimed that while they had not actually met Hughes, they had corresponded with him extensively – until Hughes told national news reporters the following year that it was all a tissue of lies and McGraw-Hill stopped the presses ('the most famous unpublished book of the

20th century' is how it was described in Irving's obituary in the *Guardian* in 2017). Irving and Suskind paid back the advance and went to prison. Irving still got a book out of it, since he then published *The Hoax* in 1977 which detailed the entire crime, and a film of the same name was made in 2006 in which he was played by Richard Gere.

When, though, is a fake not a fake? Binjamin Wilkomirski recounted his childhood in Nazi concentration camps in his 1996 book *Fragments: Memories of a Childhood, 1939–1948*, and became an international publishing sensation on the back of it. His memoir was demolished three years later when it turned out that his infant years were not spent in Auschwitz but in an orphanage and then with adoptive parents in Switzerland, learning the clarinet under his real name, Bruno Dössekker. Consequently, an entire condition was named after him – the Wilkomirski syndrome – to describe people who claim to be Jewish survivors of the Holocaust. However, even when confronted with the truth, Dössekker/Wilkomirski continued to deny he had invented anything and seemed to sincerely believe his own story. The case of J.T. Leroy also shows that there are grey areas when it comes to hoaxing. Leroy wrote memoirs about the abuse he suffered in his childhood. But he turned out to be the pen name of American writer Laura Albert, who went to significant lengths to keep the deception up, even recruiting her brother's partner to dress up for the fictional role for public appearances.

Sitting somewhere between hoax and hilarity is the story of Baron Munchausen. The real-life German baron was an eighteenth-century soldier, nobleman and teller of extraordinary tales. But his countryman and writer Rudolf Raspe published a humorous book in English of his fictionalised adventures in 1785, *Baron Munchausen's Narrative of His Marvellous Travels and Campaigns in Russia*. Although such episodes as trips to the moon were clearly not meant to be taken seriously, some readers believed they were written by Munchausen, and the baron himself certainly did not find them funny, as he felt they ridiculed him. A threatened libel suit never bore fruit, not least because Raspe wisely wrote it all anonymously.

Some fakes are very much just for personal laughs. Charles Dickens had a fake bookcase made up at his home featuring convincing spines for volumes such as *Noah's Arkitecture*, *Jonah's Account of the Whale* and *Cats' Lives* (in nine volumes). The poet Thomas Hood did something similar for the library at Chatsworth in 1831, and his work was continued there in the 1960s by travel writer Patrick Leigh Fermor, who came up with the likes of *Consenting Adults* by Abel N. Willing, and *Sideways through Derbyshire* by Crabbe. Mindell Dubansky, a senior librarian at the Metropolitan Museum of Art in New York, has collected objects that look like books for decades and named them 'blooks', curating several major exhibitions on the subject which feature book-shaped flasks, cigar boxes and spice racks.

While it is generally accepted that fakes are a 'bad thing', some good can still come from them. Arthur and Janet Freeman put together a collection of more than 1,700 volumes of literary fakes known as the Bibliotheca Fictiva, acquired in 2011 by John Hopkins University. It is impressively all-encompassing, covering what Arthur described as 'the entire range of literary forgery, that is to say the

forgery of texts, whether historical, religious, philological, or "creatively" artistic, in all languages and countries of the civilized Western world, from *c.*400 BC to the end of the twentieth century'. It includes famous forgeries such as the horrifically anti-Semitic *The Jewish Peril: Protocols of the Learned Elders of Zion* (published in Russia in 1903, fully debunked in the 1920s) as well as less well-known ones, such as *Letters from Mr Fletcher Christian* from 1796, which was supposedly the autobiographical writings by either the lead mutineer from the 1789 mutiny on HMS *Bounty*, or just as spuriously written by the poet William Wordsworth, a distant cousin. You can find a large selection of the digitised titles online at archive.org/details/bibliotheca_fictiva

As anybody who has ever spent time with an advocate of the theory that Sir Francis Bacon/the Earl of Oxford/Christopher Marlowe/an entire writing collective wrote Shakespeare's plays can testify, the world of words is also no stranger to ludicrous conspiracy theories. So no, Lewis Carroll was not Jack the Ripper and did not hide his guilt in plain sight in various of his works using ludicrous anagrams, as Richard Wallace's entirely debunked 1996 book *Jack the Ripper: Light-Hearted Friend* suggests. And it's a bit of a stretch to side with Philip K. Dick, who suggested in a letter to the FBI in 1974 that Stanislaw Lem was actually a committee of communists engaged in a shadowy propaganda war rather than a bestselling Polish science fiction writer (J.K. Rowling has also been charged – by a Norwegian film-maker – with being a literary workshop rather than a person). The committee's goal was apparently 'to gain monopoly positions of power from which they can control opinion through criticism and pedagogic essays' and it constituted 'a threat to our whole field of science fiction and its free exchange of views and ideas'. There were no hard feelings. Lem regarded Dick – who at the time of his denunciation was having drug issues – as the only competent American sci-fi novelist.

Perhaps you didn't realise that Charlotte Brontë poisoned her sisters and her brother? Yep, it's true, although she didn't work alone, recruiting her father's assistant curate Arthur Bell Nicholls to help her in her diabolical murder spree before it all went wrong for her and he ended up poisoning her. Told in novel form, crime writer James Tully's *The Crimes of Charlotte Bronte: The Secret History of the Mysterious Events at Haworth* (1999) explains that tuberculosis was not responsible for the deaths and the motive was clearly to inherit the royalties from their works. Er …

Stella Gibbons also poured scorn on the tediously common 'she's a woman so she couldn't possibly have written it' line of reasoning in her *Cold Comfort Farm* (1932) in the form of the dotty Mr Meyerburg, who is keen to expound on the not uncommon real-world theory that Branwell Brontë wrote *Wuthering Heights* (one that was definitively proven unsound in 2020 by experts using early AI-style stylometry to prove that actually Branwell was the least likely Brontë to have ghosted the novels). Meyerburg's 'explanation' has also been used to discredit Jane Austen (whose works were apparently written by her sister-in-law Eliza de Feullide) and Mary Shelley (it seems Percy wrote *Frankenstein*) as well as more recently Harper Lee (no, Truman Capote did not write *To Kill a Mockingbird*).

Some conspiracy theories also rely on the plagiarism card. The novel *A Sucessora* by Brazilian writer Carolina Nabuco was published in 1934. It focuses on a young woman who has recently married a widower and only then realises that the memory of his dead wife constitutes a powerful threat to her own happiness. There's also a big fire in the house. Yes, it sounds a bit like Daphne du Maurier's 1938 novel *Rebecca* and there were various (entirely unsubstantiated) suggestions that the English writer's publishers had somehow come into possession of Nabuco's work, translated by her into English, and then sent it on to Du Maurier. The *New York Times* even ran an article comparing the two, prompting Du Maurier to write a letter to the newspaper, published in February 1942, denying any accusations of pinching the plot.

Another big hitter accused of literary light fingers was Sir Arthur Conan Doyle, whose cunning error was dedicating *The Hound of the Baskervilles* to the chap he'd stolen it from.

> *MY DEAR ROBINSON: It was your account of a west country legend which first suggested the idea of this little tale to my mind. For this, and for the help which you gave me in its evolution, all thanks.*

Robinson was his friend the *Daily Express* editor and writer Bertram Fletcher Robinson, who introduced Conan Doyle to various legends involving ghostly black dogs, especially Black Shuck in Devon. He also helped Doyle with other Sherlock Holmes stories before dying in 1907 aged thirty-six, probably of typhoid. Or was he poisoned with laudanum by Conan Doyle, who was having an affair with his wife Gladys and wanted a grudge-nursing Robinson out of the way? Amateur historian Rodger Garrick-Steele certainly thought so and outlined his hunch in his exposé, *The House of the Baskervilles*, in 2004. The Sherlock Holmes Society described it all as 'ludicrous'.

Here are some other questions to which the answer is 'no!':

### Was Albert Camus killed by the KGB?

The French author of *L'Étranger*, *La Peste* and *The Myth of Sisyphus* was killed in a car crash in 1960. Fact. But, suggested Giovanni Catelli in his 2019 book *The Death of Camus*, instead of the official verdict that it was accident, was it *actually* because Soviet agents had mucked about with the tyre of the car in which he was travelling so that it would burst when driven at speed? Motive? Camus had criticised the Soviet foreign minister (um, three years earlier) and the crushing of the 1956 Hungarian Revolution, and supported Boris Pasternak whose *Doctor Zhivago* was banned by the Soviet authorities. The theory was supported by novelist Paul Auster, who wrote the book's foreword. Perhaps the least ridiculous theory on this list, but still.

### Has the poem 'The Night before Christmas' been wrongly attributed to Clement C. Moore?

Officially 'A Visit from St Nicholas', the familiar festive verse was first published anonymously under the title 'Account of a Visit from St Nicholas' in 1823 in the *Troy Sentinel* newspaper in upstate New York. Fact. Everybody has assumed it was written by Clement Clarke Moore because he said he had, owned several handwritten manuscript copies of it, and only asserted his authorship when another newspaper accidentally attributed it to a Joseph Wood. However, the descendants of Moore's friend Major Henry Livingston Jr claimed he had written it for the Livingston family, even though Livingston himself never suggested anything of the kind and despite there being no corroborating evidence. If you want to go down this wormhole, try *Who Wrote 'The Night Before Christmas'?: Analyzing the Clement Clarke Moore vs. Henry Livingston Question* by MacDonald P. Jackson, the most recent anti-Mooreist.

### Was *A Christmas Carol* actually written by an American couple?

This is a one-person theory conceived by Stephen Sakellarios, from Portland, Maine, who believes that Charles Dickens stole the story of Scrooge et al. from a married couple from Boston called Mathew Franklin Whittier and Abby Poyen Whittier who had written it some years earlier. He also argues that Edgar Allan Poe did the same with 'The Raven', as did Elizabeth Barrett Browning. Mr Sakellarios also claims to be Whittier's reincarnation.

### Did somebody else write Anne Frank's diary?

Perhaps one of the most unpleasant conspiracy theories, promulgated by anti-Semitic writers in the 1950s who argued that *Diary of a Young Girl* was partly written in a ballpoint pen not available until after the war (entirely untrue), that she had never existed (disproved by testimony from the man who arrested her), and that the whole thing was a forgery or written by her father Otto (refuted by matching the handwriting to letters which were written by Anne).

### Did the CIA murder Hunter S. Thompson?

*Fear and Loathing in Las Vegas* author Thompson came across evidence proving the US government had been involved in the 9/11 bombings so the CIA took him out, faking his suicide before he could tell the world. There's not much evidence for this, in truth.

### Was Geoffrey Chaucer murdered on the king's orders?

This was the theory posited by *Monty Python* comedian and amateur historian Terry Jones, who wrote a book called *Who Murdered Chaucer?*. Did Henry IV have him killed in 1400 for political reasons? Did the enemies of Henry's predecessor Richard II kill him for his associations with the previous regime? Did

Archbishop of Canterbury Thomas Arundel have him killed because of Chaucer's attack on venal ecclesiastics in *The Canterbury Tales?* Even Jones sounds not entirely convinced of the alleged cover-up story.

«9»

# NASTY

***That arsenic is a deadly poison is an admitted fact.***

*SHADOWS FROM THE WALLS OF DEATH*, BY DR ROBERT CLARK KEDZIE

**Sociobiologist Edward O. Wilson** defined a magnum opus as 'a book which when dropped from a three-story building is big enough to kill a man'. Although history is not littered with examples of warlords bludgeoning each other to death with hefty hardbacks or rolled-up trade paperbacks, books have been vital propaganda weapons for centuries.

An exhibition at the literary Grolier Club in New York in 2023 posed the question, was the US military in the Second World War the best-read army in the world? It is certainly a contender for the title. The Victory Book Campaign run by the American Library Association and local community libraries brought around ten million books to troops around the globe. Meanwhile, US publishers went the extra mile by joining forces as the Council on Books in Wartime and bringing out special pocket-sized paperbacks called Armed Services Editions. These were light but hardy, and ran over two columns per page, enabling anybody in the forces to get stuck into *The Great Gatsby*, *Candide* or *Forever Amber* (abridged).

Though more of a defensive than offensive piece of weaponry, the Book Bloc serves as both physical armour and literary statement. This DIY riot shield designed in the form of oversized covers of literary blockbusters such as *Moby-Dick*, *Don Quixote* and inevitably

Chuck Palahniuk's *Fight Club* was on view during the student demonstrations in Rome and London in 2010, making the topic of education cuts clear as well as protecting against baton attack. A similar use of weaponry to make a cultural point is activist-artist Raúl Lemesoff's *Arma de instrucción masiva* (or *Weapon of Mass Instruction*), constructed in 2015. Lemesoff transformed an old 1979 Ford Falcon into a vehicle that looks far more like a tank in order to drive around Buenos Aires peacefully offering his stock of around 1,000 books to passersby.

That said, things could get tasty if you're packing Uwe Wandrey's *Kampfreime* (*Combat Rhymes*), which was published in Hamburg in 1968. Just the right size to fit into your pocket (as long as said pocket measures a bit more than 6cm by 13cm), the text is a series of useful rhyming chants laid out thematically, including sections on work, school and the media to bring out on student demonstrations in Germany such as the to-the-point 'Scheisst auf deutsches Vaterland/Rekrutiert den Widerstand' ('Shit on the German fatherland/Recruit the resistance'). But it's also built for direct action, since it is bound within sharp metal covers which could do some serious damage to anything in their path. Some editions include a stamp on the front which says 'Notwehrtauglich' ('justifiable self-defence'). To be honest, it's more of an artists' book, a statement about the importance of protest, which is more handy for scraping off posters than as an armament.

Books can certainly maim. In *Books Do Furnish a Room*, the tenth in Anthony Powell's *Dance to the Music of Time* novel sequence, literary critic Lindsay Bagshaw accidentally pulls down a massive bookcase onto himself while trying to confirm a quotation in

Palgrave's *Golden Treasury*. In a sad example of life imitating art, Hong Kong bookseller Law Chi Wah, proprietor of the Green Text Book Store, died in 2008 when a bookcase packed with boxes of books fell on top of him in a warehouse. It was a fortnight before he was found.

Far more likely to cause you permanent bodily harm is a series of books being hunted down by the very worthy but worryingly titled Poison Book Project, a collaboration between Winterthur Museum, Garden & Library and the University of Delaware. Among those to have been named and shamed is Leeds Central Library's innocent-looking copy of *My Own Garden: The Young Gardener's Yearbook*, published in 1855. This gentle tome, a present to Caroline Gott from her father William, a leading Leeds-based industrialist of the day, contains many tips for junior horticulturalists and has a lovely emerald green cover – which is fine to look at but not lovely to touch, since its vivid hue is down to the large quantities of arsenic used in its production, enough of which, if consumed, can prove fatal. It's not as rare a find as you might hope. The Poison Book Project's mission is to hunt down and identify books which were created using heavy metals, such as arsenic, or other lethal compounds, whether that is in the covers, endpapers or spine labels. They are surprisingly common in books of every genre – especially Victorian ones in Britain and North America which came out between the 1840s and 1860s – even though the people producing them realised that substances like arsenic were risky and could be ingested accidentally by pets as well as people. A small amount goes a long way, making it more dangerous for children than adults. So eating such a book would kill you, while licking it or sticking it in your mouth would be a very poor idea indeed (as anybody who's read Umberto Eco's *The Name of the Rose* will know ...), but even just touching your face while reading such a volume could cause complications. The arsenic transfers even if you don't see any splashes of green on your skin.

Perhaps the most lethal volume was one raising the alarm about the issue. While writer and wallpaper designer William Morris was unconvinced ('As to the arsenic scare, a greater folly it is hardly possible to imagine,' he said), in 1874 concerned Michigan chemist Dr Robert Clark Kedzie felt so strongly about the potential danger that he wrote the scarily titled *Shadows from the Walls of Death*. This put the case for getting rid of all arsenic-pigmented wallpaper as strongly as possible in the eight-page introduction, which was then followed by eighty-six actual swatches of it on sale in shops in the Michigan area. Laudable though Kedzie's intentions were, the 100 copies he had published and sent to libraries as a warning were absolutely deadly. Most of the libraries destroyed them and only half a dozen are believed to be extant today, all locked up safely and out of harm's way, although online digitised versions are available.

Lead is another no-no. It has a long history as a base for white pigment, including in paints and make-up, but is a neurotoxin: repeated exposure can lead to illness ranging from headaches to coma and full death. It is also handy as a drying agent so was often used in the binding of books, too.

It's not just the white stuff. Vermilion was popular among those looking for a striking red, for example in medieval illuminated manuscripts. Lovely to look at and with an outstanding name, for sure, but it is made from the mineral cinnabar, which chemically speaking has the less appealing name mercury sulphide and is toxic, though a bit less of a worry than arsenic.

More recently, you'd be surprised how many books have been bound in asbestos, not famously a healthy construction option. A limited first edition of Ray Bradbury's *Fahrenheit 451* – a story about mind control via burning books – was published in addition to the regular trade edition in 1953 by Ballantine Books in New York, with a signed bookplate confirming that they were 'bound in Johns-Manville Quinterra, an asbestos material with exceptional resistance to pyrolysis' (i.e. fireproof). Also enjoying a reasonably arson-proof binding were twenty-six asbestos-bound signed copies (marked 'A' to 'Z') of Stephen King's 1980 novel *Firestarter* (former drug user and his daughter who has a special pyrokinesis power go on the run from shady government agency). This edition from Phantasia Press was bound in an aluminium-coated asbestos cloth that apparently still warded off flames but without all the usual unpleasant side effects. There is some speculation that only twenty-five copies are still extant because one was destroyed in a fire...

There are other bindings and book materials that many will find distasteful. As Hamlet asks Horatio, 'Is not parchment made of sheepskins?', to which Horatio accurately responds, 'Ay, my lord, and of calves' skins too.' He could have added that goatskin is also used in the production of vellum and parchment. Similarly, a twelfth-century copy of the book of Genesis held by the British Library but originally from Rievaulx Abbey in Yorkshire appears to have been covered in fur, probably sealskin. Corpus Christi College in Oxford has a volume of religious texts from around the same period, covering the early beginnings of Cistercian monasticism in northern England, which again is bound in sealskin.

Analysis in 2025 of DNA found in medieval book coverings from European abbeys was also confirmed as harbour, harp and bearded sealskins which came from the northwestern Atlantic Ocean via Norse tradesman. While it is not clear exactly why this unusual material was used, the researchers suggested that it could be that since Cistercians liked the colour white, it was an aesthetic choice.

And right at the furthest end of the unwholesome bindings spectrum is anthropodermic bibliopegy, the practice of using human skin to bind books. There are very few confirmed examples of this, though Surgeons' Hall Museums in Edinburgh has a notebook covered in the skin of William Burke – half of the nineteenth-century murder duo Burke and Hare – sourced following his execution and public dissection by Professor Alexander Monro. The small notebook has the title in gold text 'BURKE'S SKIN POCKET BOOK' on the front cover and space for a pencil inside. The Boston Athenaeum owns another example, a copy of *The Highwayman: Narrative of the Life of James Allen Alias George Walton*. American highwayman Allen asked that this copy of what is essentially a deathbed confession, told to the governor of the prison where he was being held, be bound in his own skin and then given to a Mr Fenno, who had resisted robbery and who Allen felt deserved recognition for bravery. Fenno used it to spank his children when they misbehaved.

Harvard Library took a different approach in 2024, removing the human skin from the binding of its copy of French novelist and poet Arsène Houssaye's 1879 *Des destinées de l'âme* (*Destinies of the Soul*). Its owner, French doctor and book collector Dr Ludovic Bouland, bound the book at some point in the 1880s with skin he took without consent from the body of a dead female patient in a hospital where he was working. Following an investigation into the book's history, Harvard described the volume's origins as 'ethically fraught'.

«10»

# PUBLISHING

*Publishing is a terrible invasion of my privacy.*

J.D. SALINGER, *NEW YORK TIMES*, 1974

**All writers know** that the easiest way to find a spelling mistake in your work is to write several drafts, carefully check the final manuscript, make sure several copyeditors and indexers also look closely at it, then once it is printed open up a copy on publication day randomly and you will immediately find an error. It's understandable. We are all human. Nobody's prefect.

So the unnamed father sees his son walking along a bench instead of a beach in Cormac McCarthy's *The Road*, and the 1961 first edition of Henry Miller's *Tropic of Cancer* was full to the brim with examples (it's marked 'Very Sloppy' on Book Errata's online compendium of examples), such as 'maps of Paris before the plauge', 'mythical cratures', and 'he listend to me incomplete bewilderment'. Even dictionary editors can have a bad day. The 1934 *Webster's New International Dictionary* included the word 'dord' and defined it as 'density'. Actually, it came from an editor's note that density could be 'D or d' in abbreviated form. It was five years before anybody noticed this 'ghost word', thirteen before it was finally taken out.

It's not hard to imagine the collective red faces of those who allowed the first edition of Tracy Chevalier's *Girl with a Pearl Earring* to come out with the spelling of the key item as an 'earing' on the back cover. This also happened to *Harry Potter and the Philosopher's Stone*. Not only did the 1997 first printings have an unwanted '1 wand' on page 53, but 'philosopher' also appeared on the back cover without the second 'o'. It's a good job that the publisher checked the uncorrected proof copy, though, because the title page had her name as J.A Rowling. It's even more important to check, recheck and check again when it comes to self-publishing, since fewer eyeballs are likely to look at the text.

When Taylor Swift self-published her *The Eras Tour Book* in 2024, readers pointed out various mistakes including the song 'this is me trying' appearing as 'this is me rying', plus various other spelling and grammatical faux pas. Various wags christened it *The Errors Tour Book*.

Ages can get mixed up, too. In *Charlie and the Chocolate Factory*, Roald Dahl very specifically says that Grandpa Joe is ninety-six (and a half) and indeed that 'every one of these old people was over ninety'. But in the sequel, *Charlie and the Great Glass Elevator*, Grandpa Joe requests that after some age-changing shenanigans Grandma Josephine be returned to her proper age, which is eighty. He's not just being gallant because Grandpa George is also said to be eighty-one, and Grandma Georgina just seventy-eight.

The numbers also seem not to add up for Jules Verne in his *Around the World in Eighty Days*. Here's the meeting early on in the book between Phileas Fogg and Passepartout:

> *'Passepartout suits me,' responded Mr Fogg. 'You are well recommended to me; I hear a good report of you. You know my conditions?'*

> *'Yes, monsieur.'*
>
> *'Good! What time is it?'*
>
> *'Twenty-two minutes after eleven,' returned Passepartout, drawing an enormous silver watch from the depths of his pocket.*
>
> *'You are too slow,' said Mr Fogg.*
>
> *'Pardon me, monsieur, it is impossible—'*
>
> *'You are four minutes too slow. No matter; it's enough to mention the error. Now from this moment, twenty-nine minutes after eleven, a.m., this Wednesday, 2nd October, you are in my service.'*

Despite some valiant attempts by commentators to explain those missing minutes (exactly the same times are in the French original, so nothing has been lost in translation), involving the length of the conversation and the margin of error in watches of the time, it feels like it simply does not add up. Or perhaps it's simply something unusual about timekeeping in London, because at the end of the book, when the pair have finished their world tour, 'Mr Fogg stepped from the train at the terminus, all the clocks in London were striking ten minutes before nine', which is a most unusual time for them to do so.

Questions must also be raised about how Fogg also manages to make his timeline mistake (he should have noticed the day change in San Francisco, and that there was a tremendous hustle and bustle on the streets of London for a supposed Sunday), as they must also about a central plank in Ian Fleming's *Goldfinger*. In brief, the eponymous villain seems to have horribly underestimated the weight of gold he plans to whip from Fort Knox, an issue the film sought to correct by swapping pinching the gold to simply irradiating it for decades, which is just as wonky.

There is a crossover area when it comes to the distinction between a typo and a continuity error. In Robert Heinlein's religio-science fiction *Stranger in a Strange Land* (1961), about a human raised by Martians returning to Earth, a character called Agnes also appears to be named Alice. Similarly, Agatha Christie mixes up Hercule Poirot's sidekick Captain Hastings' wives – he is about to marry Dulcie at the end of *The Murder on the Links*, but by the time of *Peril at End House* it is Dulcie's twin sister Bella who is the lucky lady, even though she has married another character, Jack Renauld. Among various continuity errors in Stephen King's work is Eddie's broken arm in *It*, which switches between left and right, and a shotgun which becomes a rifle when shot by Annie at a television cameraman in *Misery*.

If it's any consolation, these kinds of things bother authors as well as readers. In 2015, George R.R. Martin conceded that minor mistakes in his *A Song of Ice and Fire* saga books, such as characters' eye colour suddenly changing, annoy him as much as readers, especially as he writes deliberate inconsistencies into the text. Not all authors mind this much. In Raymond Chandler's partly bookseller-based detective mystery *The Big Sleep*, a chauffeur is killed during Philip Marlowe's murder investigation but the reader never discovers the perpetrator. When they were turning the book into the film starring Humphrey Bogart and Lauren Bacall, the scriptwriters asked Chandler whodunnit. 'Damned if I know,' he replied.

One of the problems is that in a long and complex series of novels such as Martin's still unfinished epic it is hard to keep everything indisputably bang on. Although it is hardly a crime against humanity, J.K. Rowling's *Harry Potter* series asserts that his parents James and Lily died on a Tuesday but then later states it was 31 October 1981, which was actually a Saturday. 'As obsessive fans will tell you,' Rowling has said, 'I do slip up! Several classrooms move floors mysteriously between books and these are the least serious continuity errors!' Similarly, it is possible to nitpick about Terry Pratchett's *Discworld* books, though he inventively said there were no inconsistencies, only 'alternative pasts', and these were perhaps due to the History Monks interfering with the passage of time. Among the most popular fan theories about the issue is that some wizards are in fact able to rewrite history, which obviously has knock-on effects …

Some inconsistencies properly belong in the realm of speculation. So while avid Tolkien fans debate whether balrogs have wings (it's not conclusive, fact fans) or why Gollum said the ring was a birthday present when in fact hobbits offer gifts to other people on their birthdays, most readers would regard these as items for debate rather than mistake. Tolkien himself wrote that 'facts that may appear in my record, I believe, [are] in no case due to errors, but omissions, and incompleteness of information'. Perhaps that also explains why Arthur Conan Doyle's Dr Watson's wartime bullet wound in Afghanistan seems to wander from his shoulder (*A Study in Scarlet*) to his leg (*The Sign of the Four*) or the muddying of waters over exactly how many wives he had – anywhere from three to six, according to some counts.

Handily, George Macdonald Fraser could use both the 'deliberate inconsistencies' and 'incompleteness of information' to explain away anything spotted by eagle-eyed readers of his *Flashman* series of novels set during the Victorian era, since the central conceit of the books is that they are written by an unreliable narrator who is not privy to all the facts of the events in which he is caught up. Two examples relate to Flashman's family: his uncle Bindley switching between his mother's and his father's side of the family (making him either more highborn or more lower class than Flashman respectively), and Selina being his granddaughter (*Flashman and the Tiger*) or his great-niece (*Flashman and the Mountain of Light*).

These kinds of mistakes are nothing new – in the first edition of Daniel Defoe's *Robinson Crusoe* our hero pulls off all his clothes to swim back to his shipwreck and see what useful things he can find, then cleverly stuffs biscuit into his pockets, not to mention complaining about having no ink to write with and a page later appearing to have decent supplies of it. In fact these are sometimes called 'Homeric nods', after Horace's observation in his *Ars Poetica* that he gets annoyed when Homer nods off ('*et idem indignor quandoque bonus dormitat Homerus*'), i.e. when he is guilty of slight inconsistencies, such as when Menelaus kills Pylaemenes in a fight in the fifth book of the *Iliad* only for said Pylaemenes to turn up in the thirteenth book when his son is killed.

What is rather more serious is when an entire text is mistakenly printed. This is exactly what happened to Britain's most famous lexicographer, Susie Dent, from television's popular *Countdown* programme. When she received the first author's copy of her book *Word Perfect*, published by John Murray in 2020, she noticed there was something wrong in the Acknowledgements section and quickly realised with rising concern that there were plenty more errors.

This was not surprising since a pre-final edit version had been used in place of the fully corrected one. 'Typesetting errors' were apparently to blame when something similar happened to the UK edition of Jonathan Franzen's novel *Freedom* (insert *Corrections* pun here), which resulted in the recall of 8,000 copies. At fault was the use of an earlier draft typescript with its consequent grammar and spelling mistakes, plus some minor characterisation differences. Publisher HarperCollins even set up a recall hotline to help recompense readers who had already bought a copy.

Errata/erratum slips which corrected many of these kinds of errors in the past have largely died out now. A nice example of what could go wrong [thanks to Mark Athitakis] is shown in the slip for the edition of Marcel Proust's *Swann in Love*, which features Jeremy Irons as the cover star from the 1984 Franco-German film directed by Volker Schlöndorff. It reads:

> *Four pages have been misplaced as follows:*
> *the text on page 90 should be on page 92*
> *the text on page 91 should be on page 93*
> *the text on page 92 should be on page 90*
> *the text on page 93 should be on page 91*

No authors are exempt from errors, even holy ones. There have been some absolute shockers in the Bible. Leading the way is the 1631 edition of the King James Bible produced by London royal printers Barker & Lucas known as the Wicked Bible, which rather unfortunately in Exodus 20:14 listed among the Ten Commandments, 'Thou shalt commit adultery.'

It was certainly unfortunate for Robert Barker and Martin Lucas, who were fined £300 (roughly £50,000 in today's money, and coincidentally the same ballpark figure which it has made at auction most recently) and had their printing licence revoked. Even the Archbishop of Canterbury George Abbot piled in, and is said to have commented: 'I knew the tyme when great care was had about printing, the Bibles especially, good compositors and the best correctors were gotten being grave and learned men, the paper and the letter rare, and faire every way of the beste, but now the paper is nought, the composers boyes, and the correctors unlearned.' So much for printers, but so much for readers too, since it was a year before anybody noticed something had gone seriously wrong, probably William Laud, Bishop of London. It is also theorised that it was not simply a mistake but possibly a prank by somebody working in the printer's offices, or even potentially sabotage. Although Charles I attempted to have all the copies recalled and burnt, at least a dozen escaped the flames. There has also been speculation that later on, in Deuteronomy 5:24, 'Behold, the LORD our God hath shewed us his glory and his greatness' was rendered 'Behold, the LORD our God hath shewed us his glory and his great-asse', but no surviving copies feature this error and some serious scorn has been poured on this theory.

Unsurprisingly for a book that has been reprinted countless times, there have been many more mistakes with the Bible down the centuries. Some are less serious than others, such as the *Monty Python*-esque 'Blessed are the placemakers: for they shall be called the children of God' in the 1562 Geneva Bible, rather than 'peacemakers'. But some were rather more problematical. One

of Scotland's oldest surviving manuscripts is the tenth-century illuminated gospel book the Book of Deer, which also features the earliest text in Gaelic. It also suggests that Seth was the first man and Adam's grandpa in the Gospel of Luke. Here is a very abridged list of things that went wrong in the King James Version in the seventeenth and eighteenth centuries alone:

- 1612 Printers' Bible – What should be 'Princes have persecuted me without a cause' in Psalm 119:61 appears instead as 'Printers'.

- 1613 Judas Bible – 'Sit ye here while I go yonder and pray,' says Jesus in Matthew 26:36. Except in this version, which swaps in Judas.

- 1638 Vexing Wives Bible – Numbers 25:18 says 'for they vex you with their wives' but should say 'with their wiles'.

- 1653 Unrighteous Bible – In 1 Corinthians 6:9 there is another 'not' issue, suggesting that actually 'Know you not that the unrighteous shall inherit the kingdom of God'.

- 1682 Cannibals Bible – At the end of a long passage about what people should and should not do in Deuteronomy at 24:3 it reads 'if the latter husband ate her' when it should be 'hate her'.

- 1711 Profit Bible – Isaiah 57:12 says 'I will declare thy righteousness, and thy works: for they shall profit thee,' but once again there's a negative missing and it should be 'not profit thee'.

- 1716 Sin On Bible – a tiny letter reversal means that Jeremiah 31:34 calls on people to 'Sin on more' rather than 'Sin no more'.
- 1717 Vinegar Bible – the Parable of the Vineyard heading becomes the Parable of the Vinegar.
- 1763 Fools Bible – Psalm 14:1 inaccurately claims that 'the fool hath said in his heart there is a God'.
- 1795 Child Killer Bible – 'Let the children first be killed,' reads Mark 7:27, which is extreme compared to the correct 'be filled'.

A different kind of bible, the *Pasta Bible* by Lee Blaylock (2009), which came out in Australia, featured a recipe for 'spelt tagliatelle with sardines & prosciutto'. AI spellchecking gremlins in the works resulted in the ingredients list requiring 'salt and freshly ground black people' instead of pepper. Publishers Penguin had to pulp 7,000 copies.

PUBLIC LIBRARY
RULES

«11»

# LIBRARIES

*A circulating library in a town is as an evergreen tree of diabolical knowledge.*

*THE RIVALS*, RICHARD BRINSLEY SHERIDAN

'**Don't' has been** the key word when it comes to libraries since librarians first began reluctantly opening their doors to the public. Opening hours have been at the front and centre of library rules for thousands of years. During the reign of the emperor Trajan around AD 100 an inscription was placed on a marble block for those visiting the public Library of Pantainos in Greece:

βυβλίον οὐκ ἐξε-
νεχθήσεται, ἐπεὶ
ὠμόσαμεν· ἀνυγή-
σεται ἀπὸ ὥρας πρώ-
της μέχρι ἕκτης.

or

*No book shall be taken out, as we have sworn an oath. It will be open from the first hour until the sixth.*

The eponymous Rule of St Benedict, written 400 years later, also closely regulated library usage:

> *In Lent moreover let them each have a book from the library and read it straight through: and these books are to be given out at the beginning of Lent. And above all let one or two seniors be deputed to go round the monastery and keep observation during reading hours lest by chance any brother be found morose and idle, or chatting instead of intent upon his reading; and therefore be not only useless to himself but also a distraction to others.*

It was a three strikes and you're out sanction, because if a monk strayed thrice with his library book then 'let him be subjected to correction according to rule in such wise *that others be put in fear*' (author's italics).

Things had changed a bit by the early nineteenth century. The University of Glasgow Library only allowed readers to borrow two books. Fair enough. But these could only be taken out on Mondays, Wednesdays and Fridays, which seems a little harsh, and could only be returned on Tuesdays and Thursdays … And when it came to exactly what they could take out, there were even more challenges to the eclectic reader. A rule from 1712 still in effect more than 100 years later put strong restrictions on lending fiction to students, who were only allowed to be issued books 'proper to their present study, and none which may have a bad influence upon their principles and morals'. By the 1820s, the authorities had caved in very slightly and graciously gave the students permission to borrow novels … so long as they were printed in a foreign language. Then in 1861 they took the enormous step of granting permission to those studying English literature – although nobody else – to borrow those written in English.

Samuel Pepys included plenty of rules in his will about what should happen to his personal library of 3,000 books, or as he called it the 'Bibliotheca Pepysiana'. A codicil of 13 May 1703 included details 'For the further Settlement & Preservation of my said Library, after the death of my Nephew John Jackson' and, long story short, it had to be kept whole, in a special room in a Cambridge college, and nobody could take books out beyond the library grounds. This is his precise wording:

> *1st That after the death of my said nephew my said Library be placed and for ever Settled in one of our Universities and rather in that of Cambridge than Oxford. 2dly And rather in a private College there than the publick Library. 3d'y And in the Colleges of Trinity or Magdalen preferable to All others. 4thly And of these two Caeteris paribus, rather in the latter for the Sake of my own and nephews Education therein. 5thly That in which soever of the two it is a faire roome be provided therein on purpose for it and wholly and soly appropriated thereto. 6thly And if in Trinity, That the said room be contiguous and to have communication with the new Library there. 7thly And if in Magdalen That it be in the new building there, and any part thereof at my nephews election, 8thly That my said Library be continued in its present form and noe other books mixt therewith Save what my Nephew may add to them of his own Collecting in distinct presses, 9thly That the said roome and books so placed and adjusted be called by the name of Bibliotheca Pepysiana. 10thly That this Bibliotheca Pepysiana be under the sole power and custody of the Master of the College*

> *for the time being who shall neither himself convey nor Suffer to be conveyed by others any of the said books from thence to any other place except to his own Lodge in the said College nor there have more than ten of them at a time and that of those also a strict entry be made and account kept of the time of their having been taken out and returned, in a booke to be provided and remain in the said Library for that only purpose.*

Libraries have rules for a reason. As Richard de Bury points out in his key library-management text of 1345, *Philobiblon*:

> *You may see some froward youth slumped idly over his studies. When in winter the frost is sharp, his runny nose drips, pinched with cold, nor does he think fit to wipe it with his handkerchief until he had bedewed the book before him with this disgusting fluid … He has his nails thick with fetid filth, as black as jet, with which he marks the place when any passage pleases him … He does not fear to eat fruit or cheese over the open book, and lifts his cup up and down regardless … Almost at once he leans forward, resting his elbows on the book, and solicits a prolonged sleep to make up for his brief period of study.*

'When admitted to the use of the books contained in the Library,' starts the rules of the library at Merton College, Oxford, from 1484,'you shall, so far as the frailty of man permits, do no damage to any book, either by handling it roughly or by tearing out its pages, but you should handle the books in a seemly fashion and keep them from all harm.' It's a pithy and polite summation of what's expected of users. And the University of Glasgow Library was keen to define exactly who users were in its revised 1768 regulations, viz.: 'Students may not loiter in the library if they have nothing to do in it.'

All libraries have extensive rules about what is not allowed (which obviously makes you suspect these are all things that people have actually done in the past). Usually these are grouped together under topic headings, but sometimes it just feels like a random list, such as this one which appeared in various regional newspapers in the spring of 1930.

> *Strict rules, which have been approved by the Hertfordshire County Council, are to be imposed by the Hyde Institute Library, Barnet Vale. Library users in future must not:*
>
> - *Enter the library if their faces are offensively dirty.*
> - *Fall asleep on the tables.*
> - *Eat their lunches whilst reading papers, books, &c.*
> - *Smoke in the building.*
> - *Leave their business cards behind.*
> - *Make themselves a nuisance.*
> - *Kick or damage the furniture.*

- *Bring dogs within the portals.*
- *Tell lies to the librarian.*
- *Enter when they are in an inebriated condition.*
- *Enter if they have smallpox.*

Although it's always good to keep abreast of smallpox-based restrictions, it's trickier to see why the readers of the *Nottingham Post, Western Gazette* in Somerset and the *Taunton Courier* would have been interested in the thoughts of Hertfordshire County Council and the Hyde Institute Library in Barnet Vale.

Sometimes these lists feel like they have been very specifically put together to deal with actual incidents. Seattle Public Library's current policy about rules of conduct cautions that the following are strictly forbidden:

- *Camping on Library grounds.*
- *Moving Library furniture from where it is placed by Library staff.*
- *Using wheeled devices inside the Library or on Library grounds, except in designated areas, including use of skateboards, roller skates, bicycles, motorized or non-motorized scooters, and shopping carts that are larger than allowed by the restriction on allowable articles.*

- *Lying down or appearing to be sleeping in the Library.*
- *Gambling and group activities which are disruptive to the Library environment.*
- *Using restrooms for bathing or shampooing, doing laundry, or changing clothes.*

Restroom use is actually more of a contentious issue than you might imagine. The Central Arkansas Library System has this to say:

> *Persons who urinate or defecate anywhere on the premises other than authorized restrooms shall be immediately removed from the library and may be charged under appropriate ordinances, statutes, etc.*

Less concerning than random defecation, the Cincinatti Library in the 1890s told readers that it was 'positively forbidden to spit on the floor or on the heaters'. Or as the Carnegie Library in Alexandra New Zealand put it more technically, 'No person shall smoke or expectorate within the library.'

Some of these forbidden actions are more than mere rules: they are actually enshrined in law. The 1898 Library Offences Act made it illegal in the UK not only to 'behave in a disorderly manner' or to 'use violent, abusive or obscene language' but also to 'bet or gamble'. On top of which, it went after any such person 'who, after proper warning, persists in remaining therein beyond the hours fixed for the closing of such library or reading-room', imposing on such evildoers a forty-shilling fine. Gambling and betting have no longer been specifically prohibited since a 2005 rejig of the law, though many libraries around the world still have something along the lines of the Warren-Trumbull County Public Library in Ohio, which asks people to enjoy the library building and grounds without 'panhandling or soliciting for self or others' or indeed 'ongoing use of the library as place of commercial business'.

One of the most basic library commandments is silence. '*Non patitur quenquam coram se scriba loquentem: Non est hic quod agas, garrule, perge foras,*' suggested Bishop Isidore of Seville (560–636) in his encyclopaedic collection known as *The Etymologies*. A rather lovely translation of it by John Willis Clark in his *The Care of Books* (1901) runs:

*A writer and a talker can't agree;*
*Hence, idle chatterer; 'tis no place for thee.*

The Western University Library, Ontario, makes a pertinent additional observation:

> *Since many persons are constantly making use of the collections, quiet is essential. Think of the other students when you are in the reading room and in the corridors. Whistling in the tunnel carries up to the top floor.*

However, some issues have rather receded with time. Here we are back at Merton College again in the late fifteenth century, where Rule IV runs:

> *Likewise, if you happen to lose the Key of the Library, and cannot find it again within four-and-twenty hours, you shall then without further delay, report the loss of the Key to the Warden, or, in his absence, to the Sub-Warden.*

Sometimes, it was rather complicated when you could and couldn't ask for a book. The British Museum Reading Room's 1912 handbook for students informed them that:

> *Artificial light not being used in the Library, books cannot be supplied for the Reading Room service after 3.30 in January, February, November, and December; 4.30 in March and October; 5.30 in April and September; 6.30 in May, June, July, and August.*

Age, of course, is partly an issue: the powers that be are often zealously keen that their holdings do not corrupt the nation's callow youth. The standing committee of the British Museum Reading Room Trustees made this clear in their minutes of 21 March 1760:

> *Mr Sam Wilton of Newgate Street, a young man of about 16 years of age, educated under the Grammar Master of Christ's Hospital, having applied for leave to Study at the Museum.*
>
> *Resolved, that he be acquainted, that it is thought improper to admit him, till his return from the University, for which he is assigned.*

Sadly, there is a long history of barring people from libraries not only because of their age but also because of their race. In 1902, Andrew Carnegie continued his marvellous philanthropic library campaign by opening a new public library in Atlanta. However, scholar and African American rights activist W.E.B. DuBois, a professor at Atlanta University, pointed out that in fact a third of the state's population was unable to access it. The *Bulletin* of Atlanta University that same year reported that at a meeting of the library board its chairman made it grimly clear 'that negroes would not be permitted to use the Carnegie Library in Atlanta', adding vaguely: 'that some library facilities would be provided for them in the future'. It took nineteen years for such a library to be built.

As well as age and racial discrimination, there has been a long history of sex discrimination. Part of the 1431 rubric for the library of the University of Angers in France covers details on:

*'de non introducendo seu tenedo mulieres occasione peccati in domo librarie'* – or in English: 'on not bringing or keeping women in the library building as occasion for sin'.

Sinning in the library was certainly seen by some authorities as a very genuine problem. In the third quarter of the nineteenth century, the newspapers in Cincinnati were alight with readers' concerns that their library was not necessarily a force for good. 'There are upon the shelves of the Public Library,' argued the *Cincinnati Gazette* of 30 July 1881, 'intended for general circulation, books of an improper character full of moral poison ... the road to ruin begins, in many cases, right at the counter of the Public Library.' But worse still were fears that the library was being used for romantic assignations – or as an anonymous letter to the *Cincinatti Enquirer* forthrightly put it:

> *I am able to prove that the Library Building is frequented by prostitutes, and that it is used as a place of assignation by young girls. It is a general rendezvous for people who are on the loose. I know a number of young men who boast of the facility which the Library has afforded them in their nefarious business.*

Head librarian Thomas Vickers had a cunning plan, bringing in rules to keep men and women apart, including one that meant they checked out their books from separate desks. In his report to the Board of Managers of the Public Library in 1875 he made this clear: 'The Ladies' Delivery counter, on the north side, has a front of fifty-one feet, and the gentlemen's counter, on the south side, has a front of thirty-nine feet.' Vickers assured the board that he was not sleeping on the job generally by adding: 'During the year one person was convicted before the Police Court of this offense [persons who cut or otherwise mutilate the newspapers of the Library] and sent to the Work-house for thirty days.'

The Vatican Library is among many which tells you in no uncertain terms what items are not acceptable in its confines.

> *It is strictly forbidden to bring and use scissors, knives, razor blades, razors, matches, adhesive paper, adhesive tape, glue, ink bottles, correction fluids, and generally any kind of liquid, substance or other object which could damage the collections of the Library.*

But it goes a stage further in laying down the law about how users should actually read its books in its Manuscript Reading Room:

> *The manuscript being read or studied must always stand on the lectern and the pages should be held open by inserting the rods provided into the base of the lectern.*

> *Hands and fingers must never rest on the manuscript to follow the lines while reading, however the card provided on the lectern may be used.*

Masterton Library in New Zealand has operated a 'no hats' policy. In 2017, seventy-eight-year-old Fay Lambert contacted her local newspaper, the *Wairarapa Times-Age*, after she was asked to leave the premises for failing to take off her bright pink cap. The library's policies included a section calling for all hats to be removed so that security cameras could properly identify – and thus discourage – book thieves.

This succinct warning from the Shrewsbury Reference Library in 1886 also feels rather ominous: 'Persons giving a false name or address will be held responsible for the consequences.'

Over time a rather less oppressive series of fines has been established, sometimes in considerable detail, such as the second of these laws for borrowers from an 1801 '5 Laws for Library Borrowers' bookplate from a library in Farmington, Connecticut:

1. *Two pence per day for retaining a book more than one month.*

2. *One penny for folding down a leaf.*

3. *Three for lending a book to a nonproprietor.*

4. *Other damages appraised by a committee.*

5. *No person allowed a book while indebted for a fine.*

«12»

# CENSORSHIP

***He who destroys a good book, kills reason itself.***

*AREOPAGITICA*, JOHN MILTON

**As long as** we've had books we've had book bans and fools in charge trying to suppress those that don't fit their worldview. Qin Shihuangdi, the first emperor of China – best known as the man who commissioned the Terracotta Army – has a decent claim to the title of Father of Book Censorship after he not only buried hundreds of Chinese academics alive in 213 BC, but also then ordered the burning of many books in his kingdom to ensure he could micromanage how history viewed him.

Of course he wasn't alone. Plato saw plenty of positives in censoring books, arguing in Book II of the *Republic* (in classicist Benjamin Jowett's iconic Victorian translation) that 'we must therefore have a censorship of nursery tales, banishing some and keeping others. Some of them are very improper, as we may see in the great instances of Homer and Hesiod, who not only tell lies but bad lies.'

Slightly more recently, the first book to be banned in the United States is commonly regarded as *New English Canaan* by the early colonist Thomas Morton in 1637. The local Puritan authorities felt this satirical work of history was overly critical of, well, the local Puritan authorities. And book censorship has not gone out of fashion since then, far from it – the last book to be banned in the UK was David Britton's most unpleasant *Lord Horror* in 1991 on grounds of obscenity, though an Appeal Court ruling the following year saw the ban lifted.

The United States has seen growing numbers of bans and challenges, including some which induce more than usual eyebrow raising. Kern County banned John Steinbeck's *The Grapes of Wrath* following a campaign by the Associated Farmers of California, who objected to how farmers were portrayed (it was allowed back on shelves in 1941). *Where's Waldo?* got into trouble for a while in 1987 when a partially lowered bathing suit top was, despite being barely visible, sufficient to incur bans in Michigan and New York until author artist Martin Handford made the most minor of adjustments. Even more unlucky was the 1967 children's picture book *Brown Bear, Brown Bear, What Do You See?*, written by Bill Martin Jr and illustrated by Eric '*Hungry Caterpillar*' Carle. An over-zealous 2010 Texas State Board of Education banned it on the basis that Martin was also the author of *Ethical Marxism: The Categorical Imperative of Liberation*, a survey which they felt was overtly anti-American. Except the Board had not done its research properly/at all and had mixed up two entirely different Bill Martin Jrs.

Among the many people fighting back against book bans is Margaret Atwood, whose novel *The Handmaid's Tale* (1985) has had a torrid time with numerous challenges. Her publisher Penguin Random House produced an unburnable copy of the book with foil pages sewn together with nickel wire, a dust jacket made out of thick aluminium, and plenty of high-temperature adhesive – Atwood even had a go at it with a flamethrower, which did no

damage. It was sold at auction by Sotheby's for $130,000 in 2022 to raise money for literary freedom campaigners PEN.

Here are some of the various reasons why titles have come unstuck in modern times, from tyrannical governments and the Inquisistion all the way up to mothers.

### Anti-Semitism: *The Metamorphosis* by Franz Kafka

Franz Kafka couldn't catch a ban break with either the Nazi regime or the Soviet Union: the former regarded his work as degenerate, and the latter as decadent.

**Official Secrets Act: *Spycatcher* by Peter Wright and Paul Greengrass**

The former MI5 officer Wright was pretty damning about the British intelligence agencies, particularly MI5's Director General Sir Roger Hollis, whom he accused of being a Russian mole. The British government's efforts to prevent publication in 1987 on the grounds of security were not only unsuccessful (the courts ruled it was fine for sale the following year) but ludicrous, since it was easily available not only in various countries around the world but also Scotland.

**Obscene Publications Act: *Lady Chatterley's Lover* by D.H. Lawrence**

We've already seen Lawrence having a rotten time in court over his novel *The Rainbow*, and he had various other issues with the authorities: his poetry collection *Pansies* was intercepted by the Post Office, which went through his private post, and an exhibition of his art was raided by the police. His most famous brush with the law came with the publication of *Lady Chatterley* and a subsequent trial for obscenity. After various experts spoke on behalf of publishers Penguin – though not Enid Blyton, who declined to do so – the verdict was not guilty.

The times they have a-changed, though – in 2019 the government put an export bar on the copy the judge, Sir Laurence Byrne, used and annotated in the original case to prevent it from being sold overseas. Byrne's copy – which also features his wife Lady Dorothy's thorough underlining of the rudest passages and notes such as 'coarse' – was eventually acquired by Bristol University.

### Extramarital sex: *The Stud* by Jackie Collins

Both this 1969 novel and *The World Is Full of Married Men*, which came out the previous year, were banned in Australia and South Africa. Just for good measure, prolific romantic novelist Barbara Cartland called the book nasty, filthy and liable to create perverts throughout Britain.

### Mum: *By Grand Central Station I Sat Down and Wept* by Elizabeth Smart

Elizabeth Smart's Canadian mother Louise was not at all pleased when her daughter's novel – based very obviously on her stormily passionate affair with the married British poet George Barker – came out in 1945. By now, she heartily disapproved of the highly talented Barker (who to be fair was a violent, womanising drinker) and so pulled strings with her friends in high places in Canada's government – the family's summerhouse was next to Prime Minister Mackenzie King's – to make sure that copies of the book could not be imported into the country on the basis that it dealt explicitly with sex outside marriage. When she did find any copies, she bought and burnt them, including the one Elizabeth sent her. The initial print run was only 2,000, so when copies do come onto the rare book market they fetch impressive prices.

### Political subversion: *The House of the Spirits* by Isabel Allende

Allende's 1982 novel was immediately banned on publication in her home country of Chile under the iron rule of General Pinochet, whose murderous coup included the assassination of the previous president, the novelist's father's cousin. The book has also been regularly challenged in the United States for various reasons including being irreligious and immoral, prompting Allende to write: 'I find myself in the unusual and awkward position of having to "defend" my novel *The House of the Spirits* that risks being banned from a high school in Boone, North Carolina. Banning of books is a common practice in police states, like Cuba or North Korea, and by religious fundamentalist groups like the Taliban, but I did not expect it in our democracy.'

### Talking animals: *Alice's Adventures in Wonderland* by Lewis Carroll

Unbelievably, this children's classic was banned in China in 1931 because it contained talking animals exhibiting human-like emotions, and thus, apparently, insulting all *Homo sapiens*. It's more than unbelievable, it's very possibly not true, even though Wikipedia and multiple other websites claim its veracity (in startlingly similar wording ...). The culprit in this case is an anonymous column in the

*New York Times* called 'Topics of the Times', which in 1931 asserted that the governor of Hunan province had put *Alice* on the banned list. What's true is that he did fulminate against chatty animals in fiction *in general* – but there is no evidence that he managed to have his personal prejudices officially ratified, as an article by Sen Wong in the winter 2012 issue of *Knight Letter*, the Lewis Carroll Society of North America's membership magazine, makes clear. The waters are muddied still more since the translator of *Alice* into Chinese, Y.R. Chao, suggests in his autobiography (*Family in Chaos* in the English translation) that the novel was prohibited for a year or two on the basis of encouraging superstition. Anthropomorphic pigs also briefly caused a ban for George Orwell's *Animal Farm* in private schools in the United Arab Emirates during the early 2000s.

### Bourgeois individualism: *Jane Eyre* by Charlotte Brontë

*Jane Eyre* was very popular in China in the first half of the twentieth century, first in rather abridged/bowdlerised translations as more of a soupy romance, but then in its entirety from 1949 onwards. However, during the Cultural Revolution of the 1960s and 70s it fell foul of the censors, who claimed it was unashamedly Western bourgeois literature and scoured it from mainland China. In the last forty years the tide has happily turned again, and it is now taught in Chinese schools and acclaimed as a classic.

### Lack of self-censorship: *Capital and Ideology* by Thomas Piketty

Even though China's President Xi Jinping has sung economist

Thomas Piketty's praises, he still insisted that the author make some ten pages of serious cuts for a proposed Chinese translation of his 2019 volume, especially the sections on China's income inequality. Unsurprisingly, Piketty refused.

### Greek junta: *Lysistrata* by Aristophanes

Written in 411 BC, this comedy with a serious edge about sex and war has been a popular play for the last two millennia. Because of its content it has suffered several bans, including one on posting it in the United States which lasted from the mid-nineteenth century to 1955. It also came a cropper in Aristophanes' native Greece. The conservative government of Konstantinos Karamanles had already banned a production of Aristophanes' play *The Birds* in 1959, citing religious concerns but actually because the pro-communist translator Vasiles Rotas had added in numerous anti-American jibes. And when the military junta took power in 1967, only official and sanitised productions of *Lysistrata* were allowed because of its rebellious anti-war message. George Zervoulakos's 1972 film of the play only managed to escape the censors' red pens by turning it into more of a zippy musical, though still with an undercurrent of agitation.

### Committee on Evil Literature: *Married Love* by Marie Stopes

This fabulously named agency was set up in 1926 by the Irish Free State's Department of Justice to look into immoral or sexually dubious material. In turn it established Ireland's Censorship of Publications Board three years later, which promptly put Marie

Stopes's bestseller about birth control straight onto the list, as well as her other titles *Wise Parenthood, Early Days of Birth Control* and *Radiant Motherhood*. Of course she was not alone. The list – which operated until the Censorship of Publications Act was ratified in 1967, limiting a book's ban to a dozen years – also featured Kate O'Brien (*Mary Lavelle*), Aldous Huxley (*Point Counter Point*), Radclyffe Hall (*The Well of Loneliness*), John Steinbeck (*East of Eden*), Graham Greene (*The Heart of the Matter*) and Ernest Hemingway (*A Farewell to Arms*). Talking of which ...

### Battle of Caporetto: *A Farewell to Arms* by Ernest Hemingway

Hemingway was pretty vocal about how little he thought of Italy's fascist leader Benito Mussolini, so it cannot have come as much of a shock when his 1929 novel about a young American soldier serving in the ambulance corps in Italy in the First World War was given the thumbs down and stuck on the censored list. Personal animosity aside, Hemingway's story included some harsh comments about what he saw as an inept, lazy and cowardly Italian military force, especially its disastrous performance in the 1917 Battle of Caporetto. Hemingway – who served as an ambulance driver in Italy in the First World War – always maintained publicly that the book was fiction.

### Immorality: *Fifty Shades* trilogy

Malaysia's Home Ministry did not take kindly to E.L. James's series of erotic-ish novels. In February 2015, when the books had been freely available on sale in Malaysian shops for three years, the ministry made this pretty comprehensive statement: 'The printing, importation, production, reproduction, publishing, sale, issue, circulation, distribution or possession of the publication described, which is likely to be prejudicial to morality, are absolutely prohibited throughout Malaysia.' Unsurprisingly, Malaysia banned the film versions, too.

### Nazis: *Snorri the Seal* by Frithjof Sælen

This Norwegian children's book, written and illustrated by Sælen, came out in 1941 while Nazi forces were occupying Norway. The satirical story focuses on the eponymous seal, who is pretty contented with life despite his mum pointing out that the Arctic can be a dangerous place. But then a dodgy-looking polar bear who looks a bit Russian turns up, followed by a whale with more than a whiff of the Nazi about him, and two seagulls who feel like paramilitary thugs. Uncle Bart, a kindly walrus, looks like a member of the House of Lords with tusks. Astonishingly, not only did the Nazi invaders not initially ban it, they even gave it good reviews in the Norwegian press. Then they took another look and waded in, confiscating copies and 'interviewing' Sælen, who later became a leading member of the country's resistance movement.

### No marriage certificate: *Tarzan* books by Edgar Rice Burroughs

Burroughs moved to California in 1919 where he bought some land and a ranch which he named Tarzana, after his successful series of books. The area's population gradually grew over the years, and in 1961, eleven years after Burroughs's death, a local school took his books off the shelves following objections from some parents. According to a report of the incident in the local *Southwest Times* newspaper, 'some thought there was no indication that Tarzan and his mate (Jane) were married'. Ralph Rothmund, general manager of the Burroughs estate, quite reasonably pointed out that they had tied the knot (as early indeed as the first sequel, *The Return of Tarzan*), with Jane's dad taking the role of minister having, fortunately for all concerned, been ordained some years previously.

'They were married,' Rothmund told the newspaper. 'Anyone who has read the books at all closely should know they were married. Jane and Tarzan took the marriage vows in the jungle with her father present. The father may not have been an ordained minister but after all things were primitive in those days in the jungle. Jane's father had to be – like all white men in the jungle – a jack of all trades. Such a man would be a minister, a doctor, a carpenter, anything you want to name.'

## The Spanish Inquisition: The Valencian Bible

Nobody expects translations of the Bible to perish in the flames, but that's exactly what happened to the first Bible to be translated into Valencian. Printed in 1477/8, it was one of the earliest non-Latin translations and probably the work of Bonifaci Ferrer. However, this vernacular translation was aimed at *conversos*, Jews who had converted to Catholicism, and the Inquisition became very suspicious of the whole enterprise and what it perceived as judaising elements in the text – so suspicious, in fact, that it destroyed all 600 copies, all except a single leaf which is held today by the Hispanic Society in New York City.

### Index Librorum Prohibitorum: *The Second Sex* by Simone de Beauvoir

The Catholic Church's official list of bad books was kept from 1560 to 1966; consequently it was enormously long and featured a real who's who of writers such as Voltaire, Victor Hugo and George Sand. De Beauvoir's history of the female experience published in 1949 went on the list, as it also did in a fine belt-and-braces approach by the Francoist regime in Spain in 1955. Among other works that made it onto the list were Michel de Montaigne's *Essays,* John Milton's *Paradise Lost,* Blaise Pascal's *Pensées* and Gustave Flaubert's *Madame Bovary.*

«13»

# VILLAINS

***Nobody is a villain in their own story.***
***We're all the heroes of our own stories.***

GEORGE R.R. MARTIN, INTERVIEW FOR *COLLIDER.COM*, 2011

**You have to** be careful when matching real people to potential fictional reincarnations, especially if the 'invented' character is a bit of a stinker. Real people do appear in fiction, but almost always their identities are hidden to avoid legal/physical skirmishes. Still, it's always fun to work out who is based on who in a novel, especially if the character is a thoroughly no-good swine.

To begin with, here's a baker's dozen of who's probably a bit of who:

- Norman Bates (*Psycho* by Robert Bloch) = Ed Gein, US handyman and serial killer

- Severus Snape (*Harry Potter* series by J.K. Rowling) = John Nettleship, Rowling's former chemistry teacher

- Auric Goldfinger (*Goldfinger* by Ian Fleming) = architect Ernő Goldfinger, Fleming's neighbour in London who complained about the use of his name until Fleming threatened to rechristen the character 'Goldprick'

- Professor Moriarty (various *Sherlock Holmes* stories by Arthur Conan Doyle) = American-German crime boss Adam Worth + American-Canadian astronomer Simon Newcomb + eighteenth-century London criminal and bounty hunter Jonathan Wild

- The Dalton Brothers (various *Lucky Luke* comics by Morris and René Goscinny) = the actual Dalton Gang who are supposedly their cousins

- Phyllis Nirdlinger (*Double Indemnity* by James M. Cain) = US husband-murderer Ruth Snyder

- Don Fanucci (*The Godfather* by Mario Puzo) = US mobster Ignazio Lupo

- Big Brother (*Nineteen Eighty-Four* by George Orwell) = UK's wartime Minister of Information Brendan Bracken

- Steerpike (*Titus Groan* and *Gormenghast* by Mervyn Peake) = prisoners at Bergen-Belsen concentration camp + Nazi war criminal Peter Back

- Joffrey Baratheon (*A Song of Ice and Fire* novels by George R.R. Martin) = Prince Edward of Lancaster, son of Henry VI

- Kurtz (*Heart of Darkness* by Joseph Conrad) = Congo Free State administrator Léon Rom

- Becky Sharp (*Vanity Fair* by William Makepeace Thackeray) = an unnamed governess and lady's companion in the Kensington Square area of London known to Thackeray

- Roderick Spode, 7th Earl of Sidcup (various Bertie Wooster stories by P.G. Wodehouse) = leader of the British Union of Fascists Sir Oswald Mosley

Anthony Powell's twelve-book series *A Dance to the Music of Time* offers perhaps the widest range of individuals inspired by people in real life, although arguably the only one who could be said to be a villain is Pamela Flitton, who seems to have no redeeming features at all: for example she throws the only copy of a writer's novel into a canal (boo, hiss). Powell's narrator notes 'the instant warning of general hostility to all comers that her personality automatically projected; an unspoken declaration that no man or woman could remain unthreatened by her presence'.

Pamela was based on memoirist and socialite Barbara Skelton, who was married to literary critic Cyril Connolly and then publisher George Weidenfeld, and who had numerous literary lovers including writer and editor Alan Ross, and cartoonist Charles Addams. Powell wrote in his published journals that after one of the books in the *Dance* series was published (he couldn't remember which) she wrote to him saying: 'Dear Tony, I am suing naturally, in the meantime can you advise me a good publisher for my new novel.' The sinister Dr Trelawny should also perhaps be added to the *Dance* list, since he was based on occultist and self-proclaimed prophet Aleister Crowley. Powell replaced Crowley's dictum and greeting 'Do what thou wilt shall be the whole of the Law' with Trelawny's marvellous 'The Essence of the All is the Godhead of the True', to which the correct response is 'The Vision of Visions heals the Blindness of Sight' rather than Crowley's original reply, 'Love is the law, love under will'.

Crowley was a handy inspirational figure for many twentieth-century writers when conjuring up a general portrait of evil, also providing the raw material for:

- Bond baddie Le Chiffre in Ian Fleming's *Casino Royale*
- the 'rough beast' that Yeats foresees in his poem 'The Second Coming'
- dodgy sorcerer Oliver Haddo in W. Somerset Maugham's spooky novel *The Magician*
- vengeful alchemist Mr Karswell in M.R. James's short story 'Casting the Runes'
- the devil-worshipping cult panjandrum Damien Mocata from Dennis Wheatley's 1934 black magic horror fest *The Devil Rides Out*
- the titular drug-den owner Anselm Oakes in Christopher Isherwood's short story 'A Visit to Anselm Oakes'

One of Charles Dickens's most controversial villains was the orphan pickpocket gang kingpin Fagin in *Oliver Twist*. The actual name

Fagin may come from one of his peers, a certain Bob Fagin, at the boot-blacking factory where Dickens worked as a boy and whom he recollects as being kind to him when ill in John Forster's 1872 biography *The Life of Charles Dickens*. However, Fagin's character is probably some kind of amalgam of several men. Two were well-known convicted fences, and both were Jewish. Isaac 'Ikey' Solomon, who was also believed to have run a children's pickpocket racket, was sentenced to transportation to Tasmania (though somehow avoided it after several years in prison in England) and appeared in several popular pamphlets of the day. Henry Worms had a similar criminal background and actually was forcibly removed to Tasmania, where he promptly absconded. The third is the more literary Monipodio, a criminal gang leader based in Seville in Cervantes' seventeenth-century short story 'Rinconete y Cortadillo'; he runs a reasonably similar operation to Fagin, involving younger pickpockets. Finally, there is Henry Murphy. He was sixty-ish when he appeared in London's Bow Street court in 1834, four years before *Oliver Twist* was published. Among the charges reported in *The Times* in January that year were that he and his young Artful Dodger-sounding son groomed young runaways to earn their keep by thieving.

The rotter Scrooge as opposed to the rehabilitated Scrooge in Dickens's *A Christmas Carol* may have been based on the famously miserly MP for Berkshire John Elwes (1714–1789), whom Dickens mentions in a letter listing miserly men in England, though in Elwes's case it was more a question of abstemiousness (eating out-of-date food, wearing tattered clothes, hoarding money around the home) than hard-heartedness towards others, to whom he could be generous. Another candidate is early millionaire James 'Jemmy' Wood (1756–1836), the owner of the Gloucester Old Bank and known widely as 'the Gloucester Miser' due to the stingy habits he shared with Elwes.

Another of Dickens's famous villains is Uriah Heep from *David Copperfield*. In this case, it's clear that the writer Hans Christian Andersen is a major physical inspiration. Andersen was a huge fan of Dickens and the two first met at a party in 1847, three years before *David Copperfield* appeared in print (and again a decade later, when Andersen effectively invited himself to stay for several weeks at Dickens's home in London and did not endear himself to the English author at all). As well as Uriah-style fawning over Dickens, Andersen also certainly looked like Heep, lacking eyebrows and lashes, sharing an inability to smile properly, and with a similar posture. Here's how Lady Eastlake, a prominent critic of the time (and a critic of *Jane Eyre* – 'proof how deeply the love for illegitimate romance is implanted in our nature') described the author of *The Little Mermaid*: 'a long, thin, fleshless, boneless man, wriggling and bending like a lizard with a lanternjawed, cadaverous visage ... [His] whole address and manner are irresistibly ludicrous.'

Not a bad description of Dickens's cadaverous Heep. But if Andersen was the physical muse, the villainous aspect of the character seems to have been based on Thomas Powell. Powell had been employed by a friend of Dickens, the shipping magnate Thomas Chapman, but turned out to be a forger and an embezzler who stole £10,000 from Chapman. Powell also went on the offensive against Dickens, publicly mocking his working-class beginnings in his book *The Living Authors of England*. When he emigrated to the United States, Dickens denounced him as a thief, though was forced to settle out of court when there were problems substantiating the claim fully.

Dickens was not alone in his low estimation of Powell. Poet Robert Browning, again initially a friend, wrote to various friends that Powell was 'a miserable nullity, and husk of a man' and 'a dog he repudiates for ever' as well as 'a person of infamous character – an unparalleled forger, who only escaped transporation thro' the ill-deserved kindness of his employers'. He wrote to Elizabeth Barrett in June 1846 that Powell was not to be trusted since 'his impudence and brazen insensibility are dreadful to encounter beyond all belief'.

Whether Mary Shelley's Victor Frankenstein in her ground-breaking 1818 sci-fi Gothic novel of the same name is a villain or not is up for debate, but he was at the very least terribly reckless and hugely obsessive. He's certainly not a nice person. Like Fagin, he owes his existence to several real people, including Shelley's husband Percy, who used the name 'Victor' as a pen name and in his time as a student at Eton and Oxford became hugely interested in the possibilities of electricity (he used his family as guinea pigs for experiments), chemistry and magnetism, filling his student rooms with various scientific paraphernalia. Like Frankenstein, Percy was also the offspring of distinguished wealthy parents.

Frankenstein's inspiration also owes a considerable debt to several 'proper' scientists. Italian Luigi Galvani (1737–1798), who is actually mentioned in the text, experimented with 'reanimating' the muscles of dead frogs by running electricity through them, which made their legs twitch, thus 'galvanising' them. His nephew

Giovanni Aldini took the next logical step by applying the same process to a human corpse in an 1803 demonstration using dead criminal George Forster, successfully getting the jaw to wobble, an eye to open and a hand to clench.

Sir Humphry Davy (1778–1829), better known today for his famous lamp, was active far closer to Shelley's home at the Royal Institution in London, where he gave public lectures on galvanism and chemistry. Shelley's diaries reveal she was reading Davy's thoughts on chemistry as she was writing *Frankenstein*, and some of Davy's phrasing is closely reproduced in Victor Frankenstein's ponderings on science and creation.

Finally, step forward German alchemist and dissector of dead animals Johann Dippel (1673–1734), who not only claimed to have come up with an elixir of life and to be able to swap souls between bodies, but was also born at Castle Frankenstein ...

Although Vlad the Impaler was called Dracula, it seems that this was about the only real contribution the violent Romanian tyrant made to Bram Stoker's devilish literary creation – and in early drafts not even that, since he was called Count Wampyr. The widely accepted theory is that the main inspiration was the Victorian actor Sir Henry Irving, a man known for his flamboyant performance techniques. Though technically the two men were friends, it would be nearer the mark to say that Stoker hero-worshipped Irving, who was mesmerically charming but also arrogant and demanding. Bar the fangs, he also looked rather like Stoker's description of Dracula in the book:

> *His face was a strong – a very strong – aquiline, with high bridge of the thin nose and peculiarly arched nostrils; with lofty domed forehead, and hair growing scantily round the temples but profusely elsewhere. His eyebrows were very massive, almost meeting over the nose, and with bushy hair that seemed to curl in its own profusion.*

Ironically, Stoker offered Irving the part of Dracula in the first staged reading of the work, which was held for copyright reasons just before the book was published. Irving turned it down because he said it was 'dreadful'.

Of course there are female scoundrels too. Many of Ian Fleming's rogues were based on people he knew or read about and SMERSH's shoe poisoner Colonel Rosa Klebb, in his 1957 James Bond story *From Russia with Love*, is no exception. She appears to be a mash-up of various female operatives in the Soviet intelligence services, including Colonel Zoya Rybkin – who after retirement became a hugely successful children's writer under her maiden name Zoya Voskresenskaya – as well as Major Tamara Nikolayevna Ivanova and Emma Wolff.

Among those created by Roald Dahl was the fearsome head-teacher Miss Trunchbull in his 1988 book *Matilda*. In clothing, he very specifically had horticulturalist and creator of Oxfordshire's Waterpenny Gardens Beatrix Havergal in mind, particularly her habit of wearing belted smocks over a shirt and tie, with breeches tucked into high stockings. Indeed, he even showed Quentin Blake (who illustrated the book) a photograph of her to guide his depiction, half a dozen years after her death – Dahl kept the photo in the filing cabinet of his writing shed.

In terms of character, he seems to have used childhood memories of the lady who ran the local sweet shop in his home town of Llandaff in Wales, Catherine Morgan. He called her 'mean and loathsome' in his memoir *Boy: Tales of Childhood* and his description of her as being permanently dirty, wearing a greasy apron with food and tea stains on her clothing, also suggests the problematic Mrs Twit in *The Twits*. Felicity Dahl, his widow, also suspected that the size and manner of Roald's matron at the prep school he attended in Weston-super-Mare, St Peter's, was also incorporated into the Trunchbull character.

There's far less conclusive evidence about who the manipulative Miss Havisham in Charles Dickens's *Great Expectations* was in real life. Without any direct clues from Dickens himself, various Victorian-era candidates who shared similarly unhappy marital circumstances have been suggested, including a Margaret Dick from the Isle of Wight (a favourite spot of the author's: he wrote bits of *David Copperfield* there) who coped with being left at the altar by moving her living quarters into the attic of her cottage. Interestingly, her neighbour was a Miss Haviland ... Much further afield, Eliza Donnithorne in Sydney, Australia, reacted to the non-appearance of the groom on their wedding day by also deciding to live alone, this time in her darkened house. But a sturdy link with Dickens is missing.

There are also heinous animals in fiction with human forebears. That terrible swine Napoleon the pig in George Orwell's *Animal Farm* is the porcine iteration of the Soviet dictator Joseph Vissarionovich Stalin. Meanwhile, the great white shark in Peter Benchley's 1974 beach horror *Jaws* is a fictional descendant of the shark attacks on the coast of New Jersey in 1916 which claimed various lives and also get a namecheck in Steven Spielberg's film of the book.

For some readers, it's Captain Ahab who is the villain in Herman Melville's 1851 *Moby-Dick* rather than the white whale of the title. But for those who regard the cetacean as the crook, there is a historical precursor whom Melville knew about. This was Mocha Dick, named after the Chilean island where he was initally glimpsed, a destroyer of numerous whaling ships, and escapee from dozens more in the 1830s. Explorer Jeremiah N. Reynolds described him in the May 1839 issue of the New York monthly magazine *The Knickerbocker* as 'an old bull whale, of prodigious size and strength. From the effect of age, or more probably from a freak of nature ... a singular consequence had resulted – he was white as wool!' Melville also used the sperm whale which rammed and sunk the whaling ship *Essex* in 1820, thousands of kilometres off the South American coast, as inspiration. This maritime disaster was later written up by Nathaniel Philbrick in his *In the Heart of the Sea: The Tragedy of the Whaleship Essex*, published in 2000. Incidentally, J.M. Barrie partly used Ahab as the basis of Captain Hook in *Peter Pan* – the crocodile standing in for the whale – as well as a fellow pupil when he was at Eton (name discreetly undisclosed), and perhaps a swashbuckling dash of King Charles II.

There is some discussion about whether Robert Louis Stevenson drew on his own personal experiences of cocaine and opium use for *Dr Jekyll and Mr Hyde*. Indeed there is speculation that he actually wrote the novella at speed while under the influence. Closer to home was his friend Eugene Chantrelle, a French teacher in Edinburgh who appeared to be a charming chap until it turned out he had with malice aforethought killed his wife with poison. Stevenson attended his trial, at which he was convicted and then executed, not only for his wife's murder but also for those of invitees to his dinner parties, who were served cheese on toast with more than a dash of toxic opium. Another candidate for the double life character was Edinburgh councillor, cabinetmaker and locksmith Deacon William Broadie (1741–1788), who was also an alcoholic, gambling womaniser who robbed his clients for decades before he too was caught and executed.

Stevenson's equally infamous creation Long John Silver was based on a large, jolly, bearded poet and critic friend of his, William Ernest Henley, the author of the poem 'Invictus'. He wasn't a pirate but he did have only one leg after it was amputated as a teenager following a bout of tuberculosis. In a letter to Henley in 1888, five years after the publication of *Treasure Island*, Stevenson wrote: 'I will now make a confession. It was the sight of your maimed strength and masterfulness that begot John Silver in TREASURE ISLAND. Of course, he is not in any other quality or feature the least like you; but the idea of the maimed man, ruling and dreaded by the sound, was entirely taken from you.'